137937

6

NEWFOUNDLAND AND LABRADOR

A BRIEF HISTORY

NEWFOUNDLAND AND LABRADOR

A BRIEF HISTORY

LESLIE HARRIS, PH.D.

Dean of Arts and Science
Memorial University of Newfoundland

Maps by Ross Bennington
Illustrations by Bob Teringo
Cover by Louise Parks

J. M. DENT & SONS (CANADA) LIMITED

ACKNOWLEDGEMENTS

The author wishes to express appreciation to Miss Jean A. Horwood
and Mrs. Jane Mercer for their assistance in preparing the manuscript
for publication and for their research in source illustrations.

Grateful acknowledgement is made to the following for permission
to reproduce the slides and photographs listed below:
Canadian Government Travel Bureau: 123, 164; Canadian National
Railways: 139, 145; Churchill Falls (Labrador) Corporation: 147;
The Confederation Life Collection: 23; Iron Ore Company of Canada: 148; The Memorial University of Newfoundland, Department
of Extension: 26, 28, 61, 80, 135; Miller Services: 113 top and
bottom, 161, 168 (R. J. Enns photo), 169; Miller Services and
Marshall Studios: 99 top; Miller Services and National Film Board:
99 bottom; National Film Board: 50; Newfoundland and Labrador
Department of Education: 106; Newfoundland and Labrador Department of Health: 154; Newfoundland and Labrador Provincial
Archives: 151, 165; Newfoundland and Labrador Tourist Development Office: 38, 70, 103, 116, 142, 158; The Public Archives of
Canada: 32, 66, 74, 127 ("Fathers of Confederation" by Robert
Harris); F. Wooding, courtesy of The Anglican Church of Canada:
124.

FOREWORD TO THE TEACHER

It has been a common practice to write history for children as a series of highly dramatized, highly romantic episodes or short biographies. The simple opposition of Right to Wrong and the decisive role of the Great Man have been stocks in trade. Coherence, unity, and pattern have frequently been conspicuously absent. In fact, many writers appear to believe that history can be palatable to children only if it ceases to be history and becomes fiction. If this were the case, it would be better if the teaching of "history" at the elementary level were completely avoided.

That I do not believe avoidance to be the answer is clear. Indeed, it seems obvious that there is sufficient romance and drama within the context of a significant narrative of Newfoundland's history to satisfy any reasonable thirst for excitement and adventure. But a significant narrative is crucial, for genuine history cannot be taught if we shun basic historical concepts such as explanation and multiple causation. We must assume that eleven-year-old children have intelligence and are able to think. To think historically is not more difficult than to use other forms of thought. It merely requires the proper training. To defer that training is to invite difficulties later.

This little book, then, tries to trace the major threads of Newfoundland's development from the times before Cabot's arrival to the present day. It will be clear that I have been highly selective in choosing the factual information to be presented, and equally clear that matter extraneous to a pattern of development has been rejected, dramatic though it might be. There is an intended emphasis throughout on basic concepts such as explanation, and students should be encouraged to think through such problems as why attempts at formal colonization failed while illicit settlement succeeded; why Britain refused for so long to recognize Newfoundland as a colony; why Representative Government failed; why the Commission of Government was accepted so readily in 1934; why Confederation was rejected in 1869 but accepted in 1949; and so on.

The basic approach of this book is chronological, though a departure from strict chronological sequence has on occasion been necessary. Dates, except in a few instances, have been avoided. I recognize that the concept of time is a difficult one to explain to children, and that the establishment of relationships between events and time is one of the teacher's greatest problems. Thus the mere memorization of lists of dates is a particularly fruitless exercise. At the same time, the use of key dates as "pegs" is invaluable.

Just as I have avoided the use of many dates, I have also avoided the introduction of a large number of individuals. Key figures in the history of Newfoundland must, of course, be mentioned, but their number has been deliberately kept to a minimum. Events are usually more important than the individuals who participate in them, and the number of men who actually shape events is very small. Again the emphasis is on understanding events and forces, not on memorizing names associated with events.

The teacher will find ample scope for supplementing this history. For example, the text refers to the landing of the first trans-Atlantic cable at Heart's Content and to the first trans-Atlantic flight of Alcock and Brown as significant events in Newfoundland's development because they illustrate the island's strategic position in trans-Atlantic communication. However, the teacher can supplement these data with the exciting story of the *Great Eastern* and the several cable-laying attempts, a story of scientific as well as historical interest. Similarly, the story of early attempts to fly the Atlantic should be introduced. In both cases there should be books in the school library in which the children themselves can read the exciting and fascinating details. There are many other examples, but I will mention only two: the Newfoundland seal hunt and the attempt, when it was already too late, to befriend the Beothucks. But I need not labour the obvious. No true teacher will use this, or any other textbook, as the sole source of instruction.

It will undoubtedly be found that political and constitutional arrangements are the most difficult to explain, particularly when they involve abstract principles such as responsibility. Perhaps the best way they can be presented is through the creation of a Model Parliament. Pupils can form parties, conduct elections, and form governments within the ordinary classroom. Such a device can be infinitely more effective than the best verbal presentation.

Indeed, pupil participation should be invited whenever it is feasible to do so. Sometimes it is possible to evolve community history projects that will capture active imaginations. One such project might be the construction of a map of the local area showing the place names of coves, heads, harbours, points, bays, rocks, sunkers, fishing grounds, ponds, brooks, and gullies that are not shown on any standard map or chart. When this map is completed, an attempt to establish the origins of the names might well throw interesting light on the community's past. Similarly, a collection of purely local folk songs, tales, and legends would provide an interesting and profitable project. The making of models of fortifications or fishing rooms might interest many children. The compilation of family trees might arouse the enthusiasm of others.

Above all, children must be encouraged to participate mentally. Much of the history of Newfoundland can be presented as a series of problems to be solved, of puzzles to be assembled. *How* and *why* are crucial words, and pupils should be guided to use facts not as a catalogue to be memorized, but as necessary parts of the puzzle, or as clues towards a reasonable solution of the problems.

Leslie Harris

CONTENTS

LIST OF MAPS

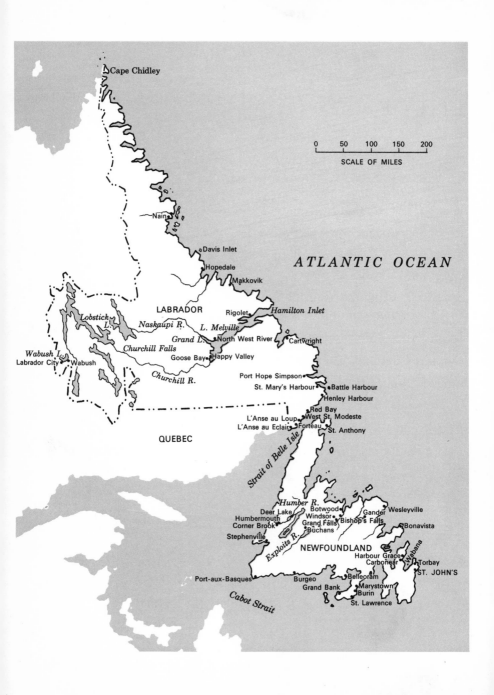

1   The Beothucks

Many years ago, long before the people of Europe discovered Newfoundland, this island was the home of a very interesting tribe of Indians called the Beothucks. They were a people who lived by hunting and fishing, by collecting sea birds' eggs and shellfish in summertime, and by picking berries and other wild plants for food.

The Beothucks were fair-complexioned and slight. Sometimes they painted their bodies, as well as their tools, weapons, and other possessions, with a mixture of red ochre and grease. For this reason they are often called "red" Indians. They were so fond of red ochre that they even used it in their hair, which they wore long and decorated with feathers and combs carved from bones.

They wore clothes made of skins. Both men and women wore the same kind of garment, which looked something like a dress. It reached just to the knees and had fringes round the hem and down the front. In winter they wore moccasins and leggings, thick mittens, and a fur collar which could be pulled up like a hood. Sometimes women carried their babies in these hoods. The furs and skins from which they made their clothing were beautifully prepared and sewed together with sinews taken from the caribou. To prepare the skins for sewing, holes were punched in them with an awl made from bone.

The Beothucks had two kinds of houses. In summer, or when

In this Beothuck village scene, notice the cone-shaped wigwams and in the background, the Beothuck canoes. In the foreground one of the men of the village is stretching out a caribou skin to dry and securing it with pegs.

they were travelling, they lived in small wigwams which could be set up very quickly. The wigwams were built of poles covered with layers of birch bark or with skins of animals. They were between six and ten feet in diameter and eight to ten feet high. Each wigwam was shaped like an ice-cream cone, with a hole at the top through which the smoke of the cooking fire could escape. Round the central fire, the ground was hollowed out and lined with fir boughs on which the Beothucks slept.

The winter homes were quite different. They were large, up to twenty-two feet in diameter, and had eight sides. The walls were made of squared logs driven into the ground and snugly fitted together. All the cracks and joins were chinked with moss and the inside wall was also lined with moss, which kept the house warm. Each house was surrounded by a bank of earth four feet high. The roof was shaped like a cone. It was covered by three layers of bark with six inches of moss between each layer. The chimney hole was lined with clay to prevent fire from breaking out. Inside the house there was a fireplace in the centre of the floor and round it were shallow pits lined with soft furs. These pits made comfortable chairs as well as snug beds. Round the walls were racks where weapons could be kept neatly, and in the loft there was space to store food.

The Beothucks lived in small groups of about forty. A winter encampment by the side of a lake or stream in the interior of the country would usually consist of two or three large houses. Each encampment would also have racks on which fish, meat, fruit, and herbs would be spread to dry. Also, many pits were dug in the earth and carefully lined with birch bark. Here the winter food supplies were stored. An encampment might also have a sweat house, that is, a special kind of wigwam in which a Beothuck who was ill would take a steam bath. To do this, he would heat rocks in the fire, bring them into the sweat house, and then pour water on them to make dense clouds of steam.

The Beothucks made pots and kettles of birch bark very neatly sewed together with tiny roots. In these containers water was boiled and meat stewed by heating rocks in the fire and dropping them into the pots. Sometimes meat was roasted on spits over the open fire. During the winter and in other times of scarcity, the Beothucks ate dried fish and meat, a kind of cake made from boiled sea birds' eggs, and a pudding made from liver, eggs, seal fat, and other ingredients.

The Beothucks got most of their meat by hunting caribou, and the great hunts required the co-operation of the entire tribe. Twice each year the caribou gathered in large herds to migrate from the north to the south in the autumn and then to return to the north in the spring. In their migrations the cari-

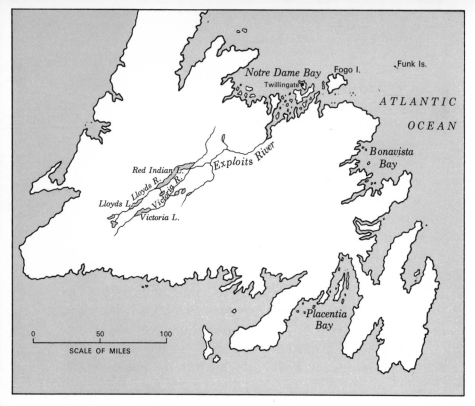

Most of the Beothucks lived in villages along the Exploits River system. In summer they visited the islands of Notre Dame Bay and the Funk Islands.

bou crossed the great rivers and lakes which the Beothucks used as their highways. For a distance of forty miles along the banks of a river, the Indians would build very high fences of felled trees. The caribou could cross the river only by first going through the small gates which the Beothucks had built into the fences. But when they passed through those gates to enter the water, the Beothucks would be waiting in their canoes with their spears and bows and arrows to slaughter them.

When enough caribou had been killed, the dead animals would be towed ashore and skinned. The meat would be removed from the bones and wrapped in birch bark in packages each weighing about two hundred pounds. These packages would then be placed in large storehouses built near the bank of the river. The storehouses were as much as forty or fifty feet long and nearly as wide. They were built of squared tree trunks and covered with birch bark and skins. Moreover, they had a ridge pole and gable ends so that they looked rather like a modern-day Newfoundland fisherman's stage.

As soon as the rivers and lakes were free of ice, the Beothucks left their winter encampments and moved along the waterways towards the sea-coasts of the island. During the summer they foraged for food along the coasts, fishing and collecting shellfish. They also journeyed to the off-shore islands to find nesting colonies of birds. Here they collected eggs and killed the adult birds for food. Sometimes they travelled as far as the Funk Islands, where the Great Auk, a sea bird as large as a goose, nested in great numbers.

The canoes in which they travelled the rivers and lakes of the interior, fished along the shore, and sometimes went out to

When men began to explore Newfoundland, they found along the riverbanks many of the fences that the Beothucks had made years earlier to trap caribou.

sea were unlike the canoes used by other North American Indians. They had the shape of two crescent moons joined at the horns. Their wooden framing was covered by birch bark sewed together with split spruce roots. They were caulked with a mixture of turpentine, oil, and ochre and ballasted with stones. On the stones, sods and moss were placed to provide comfortable cushions on which the paddlers could kneel. The canoes were between fourteen and twenty feet long and between four and five feet wide. Sometimes a sail was used, but usually the boats had only paddles or oars.

For hundreds of years the Beothucks had Newfoundland nearly all to themselves. At a very early time there had been some Eskimo settlements on the West Coast, and sometimes some Montagnais Indians from Labrador would cross the Strait of Belle Isle to hunt in Newfoundland. But usually the Beothucks could roam the country on snow-shoes in winter, paddle down the broad rivers and across the lakes, fish along the sea-shore, or hunt for deer in the autumn and spring without having to fear the presence of any enemies.

Explore and Discover

1. Do you think the Beothucks' habit of hunting along the coast in the summer led to their quarrels with the fishermen? Why?
2. Make a model of a Beothuck winter village near a stream or lake. Make a large wigwam, a storehouse, and a steamhouse.
3. Make a model of a river with a caribou fence. Find out from the Wild Life Division or the Department of Mines and Resources how caribou are captured today and taken to different parts of Newfoundland.

2 The Vikings

About a thousand years ago, hardy seafaring warriors called Vikings, or Norsemen, set out from Norway to raid the coasts of Ireland and England. But the plunder they carried home was not enough for them. Soon they set out in fleets of hundreds of ships to seize more plunder and also to find new lands to settle. Some of them settled in England and France or sailed along the coast of Spain and entered the Mediterranean Sea. Some made their way into Russia, while others turned westward and colonized Iceland and Greenland.

Most of our information about the Vikings and their voyages comes from the *Sagas*, which are old stories of Iceland. These stories tell about many explorations which the Vikings made and describe some of the places they visited. From the *Sagas* we learn that the Vikings had developed great skill in navigation and seamanship.

We can imagine their skill and courage if we think about the boats in which they sailed the North Atlantic, which is one of the stormiest oceans in the world. They were narrow, shallow boats about one hundred feet long, sixteen feet wide, and four feet deep. They had no decks, though the men were sheltered from the wind in the bow and the stern, where they slept. The boats usually had ten oars on either side, one mast, and a big, square sail that could be used only when the wind was fair. When the Vikings ran into head winds, they had to row both

In a good day's sailing, a Viking ship could cover 120 miles. Notice the carved figurehead. The shields along the gunwales protected the oarsmen from the stormy winds and waves of the North Atlantic.

night and day. They did not have compasses but steered by the stars and the sun.

Very often Viking ships were driven off course in stormy weather, and this happened to the ship of a young Viking called Bjarni one autumn about a thousand years ago. He had left Iceland to visit his father, who lived in Greenland. Storms and fogs, however, drove him far to the south. After being tossed about in the stormy seas for many days, he sighted a wooded land. He knew that this could not be Greenland because no trees grow in that country. Therefore he turned and

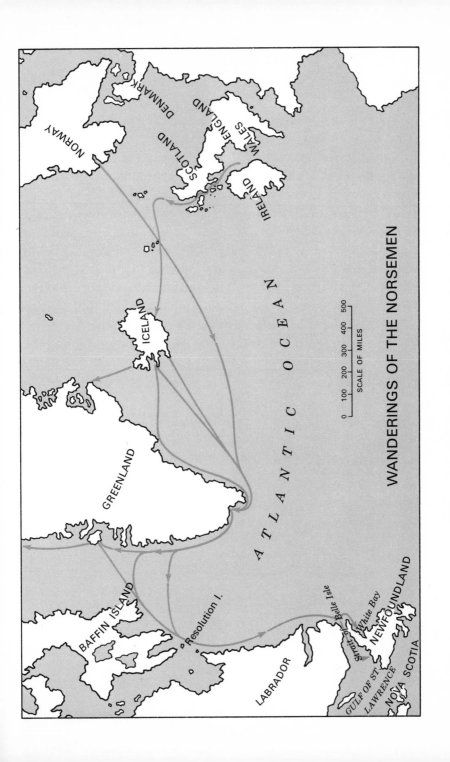

WANDERINGS OF THE NORSEMEN

sailed to the northeast and after four days came to his father's house.

The Vikings of Greenland were much excited by Bjarni's story of new lands to the southwest, and Leif Ericson, sometimes called Leif the Lucky, decided to explore them. The next spring he set sail and after some time came to a coast where a tableland of flat rocks stretched inland to snow-covered mountains. Leif called this land *Helluland*, which means "the land of flat stones". Then he sailed southward along the coast and came to a level, wooded land with broad stretches of white sand along the sea-shore. This land he named *Markland*, which means "forest land". After sailing to the south for two more days, he entered the mouth of a river which flowed from a lake near the shore. On this lake he anchored his ship. Having gone ashore and examined the site, he decided to build a

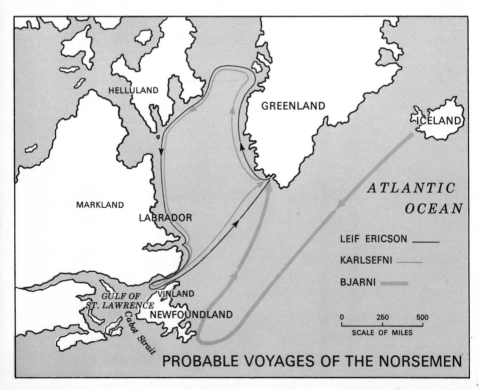

PROBABLE VOYAGES OF THE NORSEMEN

The chief weapons of a Viking were the sword and the spear. For protection he had a shield. Notice also the tools that were used to make these weapons: anvil, tongs, rasp, shears, and hammers. The Vikings were fierce fighters.

house and spent the winter there. This place he called *Vinland*, which means "vine land". In the summer Leif returned to Greenland.

The following year Leif's brother Thorvald decided to explore Vinland further. This voyage of exploration lasted three years, and during that time the Vikings made enemies of the Eskimos and the Indians whom they met on the coast of Vinland. They were attacked by the Indians, and Thorvald was killed. His crew returned to Greenland.

About ten years after the death of Thorvald, another Greenland Viking called Karlsefni decided to start a colony in Vinland. The *Sagas* tell us that the Vikings lived in the new land for five years, but, like Thorvald's men, they quarrelled with the Eskimo people and finally returned to Greenland. As far as we know, the Vikings did not try to settle in Vinland again.

For many years people have wondered where Vinland was located. After reading in the *Sagas* about the places visited by the Vikings, many people think that it was in northern Newfoundland and that Helluland and Markland were both on the coast of Labrador. Now the remains of a Viking house, which may have been that of Leif the Lucky, have been discovered at L'Anse aux Meadows. Thus it seems possible that the first white men to visit Newfoundland and to found a colony here were the Vikings. But their quarrels with the native peoples forced them to leave, and for several hundred years afterwards the Eskimos and the Beothucks were the only inhabitants of the island.

Explore and Discover

1. Draw or trace a map showing Greenland, Newfoundland, and Labrador. Mark L'Anse aux Meadows. Mark Vinland and Helluland.

2. Try to find pictures of a Viking man or woman. If you can, find a a picture of a man in ordinary clothes and also of one armed for battle.

3. Imagine that you were a Viking sailing with Thorvald to explore Vinland, and write a story of your adventures. Your story might tell what directions Leif the Lucky gave Thorvald, how your shipmates made enemies of the Indians and the Eskimos, and how Thorvald was killed in battle.

3 The Men of Bristol

During the five hundred years that followed the Viking voyages to Newfoundland, the sailors of Europe—Portuguese, Italian, Spanish, French, and English—learned a great deal about navigation and seamanship. They built staunch, seaworthy ships which could be sailed on long voyages. Although earlier ships had been rugged, they had not been able to sail to windward very well. Now the sailors learned to do without oars by rigging their ships to take advantage of the wind whichever way it was blowing. They discovered the use of the mariner's compass, which enabled them always to know the direction in which they were sailing. They also had new maps and charts and an instrument which told them how far they were to the north or south of the equator.

With the help of all this new knowledge, the sailors began to explore the Atlantic Ocean. Foremost among the explorers were the Portuguese. They pushed far to the south and west and explored the coast of Africa. They discovered such groups of islands as the Canaries and the Azores.

Stories about the new islands were told in the ports of Europe, but not all the stories were true. Often sailors told "tall tales" about rich islands and cities that they had seen far out in the Atlantic towards the west. However, many people believed the stories and soon the map-makers were making

The early Spanish and Portuguese explorers sailed on long voyages in fifty-ton ships called caravels. These ships carried four masts. Notice the square sail on the foremast and the high stern castle.

maps showing dozens of small islands scattered all over the Atlantic Ocean.

Sailors from Bristol, a port in the west of England, traded with the Portuguese and with the islands which the Portuguese had discovered. Thus they learned the arts of navigation. They also heard many legends and stories that were told about unexplored islands far out at sea. Men from Bristol also traded with Iceland, exchanging wool, cloth, and salt for fish. In Iceland they heard of the *Sagas*, and they heard the sailors tell how long ago bold Vikings had discovered Helluland, Markland, and Vinland.

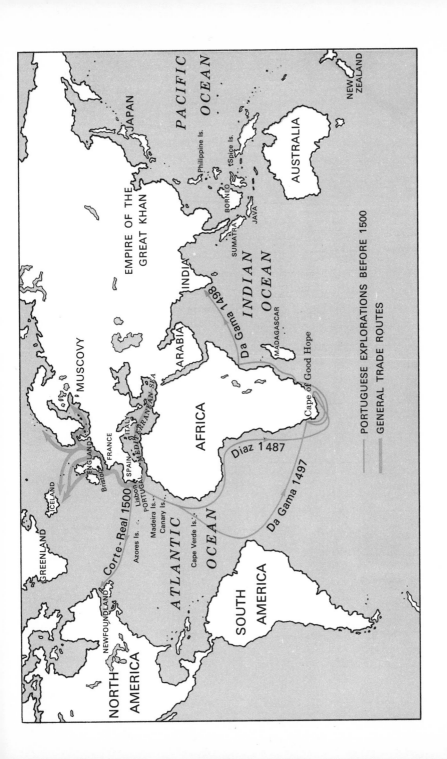

The traders of Bristol were always eager to find new lands with which they could trade. Thus they planned to send expeditions westward, hoping to find some of the islands of which they had heard or to rediscover the lands which the Vikings had colonized. The first to attempt such a voyage was a man named John Jay who, about five hundred years ago, sailed his small ship out of Bristol harbour and headed into the stormy Atlantic.

This voyage was unsuccessful, for after sailing for many days John Jay found no land and was forced to return to Bristol. But from that time on other adventurous men set out to continue the exploration. We now believe that one of those expeditions reached Newfoundland. If this was so, the sailors must have kept their discovery secret, perhaps because they did not want everyone to know about the rich new fishing grounds that they had found.

Explore and Discover

1. From what two peoples did the sailors of Bristol learn about navigation skills and the new lands to the west?
2. Imagine that you were John Jay and write a letter to a friend telling why you are going to sail westward from Bristol to look for new lands.
3. With the help of your teacher, try to find out about the lives of the two explorers shown on the map in this chapter—Da Gama and Diaz—and the voyages they made. Then write down what you have learned about each of them.
4. Imagine that you were a sailor telling a "tall tale" about rich islands in the Atlantic and write down what you might say.

4 The Age of Exploration

Five hundred years ago many people believed that the world was flat and that a ship which sailed too far might fall over the edge. But scientists and scholars had known for a long time that the world was a sphere, that is, shaped like a ball. Such men knew that it was possible to sail right around the world.

At this time traders and merchants were very eager to reach Asia and India, as well as the islands of the East Indies. These were the countries where grew spices such as pepper, ginger, cloves, and cinnamon, which were very scarce in Europe and therefore very valuable.

Of course, there were other people who were much more interested in discovery than in trade. Such people are never satisfied while there are areas unexplored, questions unanswered, or problems unsolved. They have led man from barbarism to civilization.

One such man was Christopher Columbus, who believed that if he sailed westward across the Atlantic Ocean, he would come to the rich spice islands of the East. He persuaded the King and Queen of Spain to give him money and ships to make the attempt. He sailed with three ships in 1492. As day after day passed, the sailors of his fleet saw only the ocean stretching on before them. They became frightened that they would never see their homes again. But Columbus pressed on and one morning was rewarded by the sight of land.

On reaching the New World, the *Santa Maria* was wrecked. Her crew had to make the return voyage on the *Nina* and the *Pinta*.

He had reached some islands off the coast of America, but since he did not know that the North and South American continents existed, he thought he had come to India. He therefore called the islands which he found the Indies and their inhabitants Indians. That is why to this day all the native inhabitants of the Americas are called Indians, even though they live many thousands of miles from India.

There was much excitement when Columbus returned to Spain. The news of what he had found soon spread to all the ports of Europe. Many sailors were eager to see if they too could discover new lands. Merchants were eager to reach the rich spice islands, and kings longed for new lands to rule. Countries became jealous of each other because some had new lands and some had not.

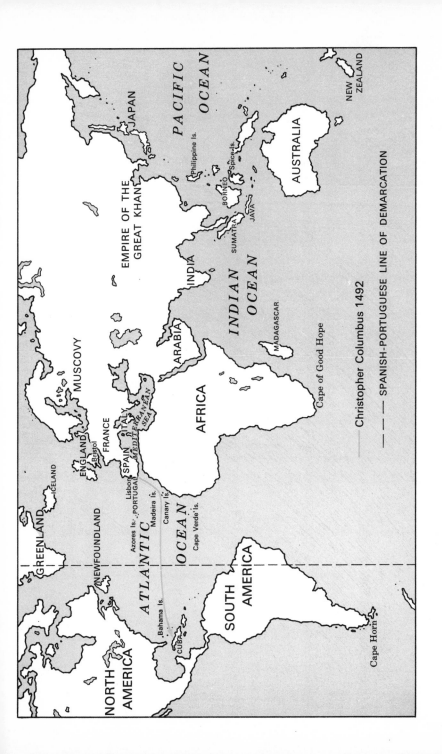

NORTH AMERICA

GREENLAND

ICELAND

NEWFOUNDLAND

MUSCOVY

ENGLAND
Bristol

FRANCE

SPAIN ITALY
Lisbon PORTUGAL
Azores Is.
Madeira Is.
Canary Is.
Cape Verde' Is.

MEDITERRANEAN SEA

ATLANTIC OCEAN

Bahama Is.
CUBA

SOUTH AMERICA

Cape Horn

AFRICA

ARABIA

EMPIRE OF THE GREAT KHAN

INDIA

INDIAN OCEAN

MADAGASCAR

Cape of Good Hope

JAPAN

PACIFIC OCEAN

Philippine Is.

BORNEO
SUMATRA
JAVA
Spice Is.

AUSTRALIA

NEW ZEALAND

———— Christopher Columbus 1492

– – – – SPANISH-PORTUGUESE LINE OF DEMARCATION

Columbus became a skilful sailor and chart maker at an early age. On his four voyages to the New World he discovered many of the islands in the Caribbean and explored part of the coasts of South America and Panama.

The greatest jealousy at this time was between Spain and Portugal. For a long time the Portuguese had been foremost in exploration. They had tried to find a route to India by sailing round Africa. Now the Portuguese feared that, because of the discoveries made by Columbus, Spain would claim lands which they wanted. To prevent the quarrel between the two countries from becoming very serious, the Pope persuaded them to share the undiscovered part of the world. A dividing line running north and south through the Atlantic Ocean was agreed upon. All new lands found to the west of this line would belong to Spain, and all new lands found to the east of it would belong to Portugal.

Explore and Discover

1. Draw or trace a map and show on it Columbus's voyage of 1492.
2. Study a globe and show how by sailing westward from Europe you could come to the east.
3. List some of the arguments Columbus might have used to persuade the King and Queen of Spain to provide him with money and ships for his voyage.
4. Think of as many reasons as you can why explorers like Columbus went on dangerous voyages and make a list of them.
5. With adhesive tape, show on your school globe how Spain and Portugal divided the undiscovered part of the world between them.

5 The Voyage of John Cabot

The agreement between Spain and Portugal did not prevent other nations from sending out ships on voyages of exploration. England was one nation that decided to do so.

At the time a skilful sailor and navigator called John Cabot was living in Bristol. He had been born in the city of Genoa, had lived for some time in Venice, and then had gone to England. He was anxious to find someone who would help him prepare for a voyage of exploration to the westward, for he, like Columbus, believed that the rich East Indies could be reached by sailing westward across the Atlantic Ocean.

In Bristol he found merchants who were willing to help him obtain a ship, provisions for a long voyage, and sailors to accompany him. Next he had to get the support of King Henry VII. The King, who was always more eager to receive money than to spend it, refused to help pay the cost of the expedition, but he did give Cabot permission to sail in whichever direction he chose, except to the south, where the Spaniards were. Cabot was "to seek out, discover, and find whatsoever islands, countries, regions, or provinces . . . which before this time have been unknown to all Christians."

On May 2, 1497, Cabot set sail from Bristol with a crew of eighteen men in a little ship called the *Matthew*. When the *Matthew* had passed the southern tip of Ireland, Cabot sailed northward for a short distance and then headed westward

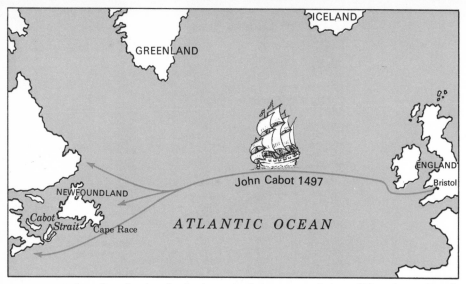

Cabot thought that he had reached the coast of Asia. When he returned, he reported that he had claimed the land he had discovered for England.

into the Atlantic. For six weeks Cabot steered a westerly course until at last, on June 24, land was sighted. Here the brave navigator went on shore and raised the flag of England and the flag of Venice. He went some distance into the forest, but finding evidence of the presence of native people, he became alarmed and returned to his ship.

Cabot now set out to explore the coast of the country which he had discovered. He sailed along the coast for perhaps nine hundred miles. Then, probably because his provisions were running short, he headed for Bristol, which he reached early in August.

In Bristol he was given a great welcome. The King rewarded him with a gift of ten pounds as well as with a pension of ten pounds per year. The people praised his skill and seamanship and called him the "great admiral". He had no difficulty in getting money and provisions for a new expedition. The following year, 1498, in command of five ships, he set sail again for the new lands. It seems that he did not return from this voyage, for that is the last report that we have of John Cabot. He may have drowned in a shipwreck or died from other causes. We are not certain of what happened to him.

What was the new land which Cabot had first sighted and on which he had raised the flag of England? This is an interesting question, but because Cabot's map and the record of his voyage have been lost, no one can be sure of the correct answer. Perhaps the landfall, that is, the place which he first sighted, was in southern Labrador, perhaps it was on the coast of Newfoundland, on Cape Breton Island, or on the coast of Nova

John Cabot left Bristol in 1497 aboard the *Matthew*. With a crew of only eighteen men, the ship sailed for many weeks across the Atlantic Ocean before land was sighted. In the painting below you can see John Cabot and his son Sebastian raising the Cross of St. George to claim the land that they had discovered for England. Note the *Matthew* in the background.

Scotia. Many Newfoundlanders have believed for a long time that Cape Bonavista was the first land that Cabot saw. In any case, we can be sure that during his voyage Cabot sailed along our coasts, and for this reason our island was called the "new found land".

Cabot, like Columbus, believed that he had reached the coast of Asia. We can imagine that he was disappointed when he found neither pearls, nor precious stones, nor the valuable spices that he had hoped to find. But although he did not realize it, he had found something which was even more valuable. He had discovered that the waters round the new land were teeming with fish. Cabot reported that they were so plentiful that his men could lower a basket into the water and pull it up filled with fish.

Explore and Discover

1. Why do you think the merchants of Bristol were willing to give John Cabot a ship and money for his voyage?

2. Why do you think Cabot believed that he had reached the coast of Asia when he sighted land?

3. As Cabot sailed along the coast of this land, what do you think he looked for?

4. What do you think was the most important discovery that Cabot made?

5. Imagine that you were a sailor on the *Matthew* and write the story of your voyage. Your teacher could help you by reading letters about the voyage from a book called *The Cabot Voyage and Bristol Discovery* by J. A. Williamson.

6 The Corte-Real Brothers

Like the men of Bristol, Portuguese sailors from the islands of the Azores wanted to find new lands across the Atlantic Ocean. They also hoped that by sailing westward they would find a route to China. One of them, a man named Fernandes, was engaged by the King of Portugal and later by King Henry VII of England to undertake voyages of exploration. Fernandes was a landowner, and in the Azores landowners were called *lavradors*. It is from this word that the name Labrador comes, although the land which Fernandes reached was really Greenland and not Labrador at all.

Another brave and skilful Portuguese sailor was Gaspar Corte-Real. He also received permission from the King of Portugal to seek new lands for the King to govern. He set sail from Lisbon in the spring of 1500 and reached the coast of Newfoundland, which he spent the summer exploring. The following year he continued his exploration, this time accompanied by his brother Miguel in another ship. But only Miguel returned to Portugal in the autumn. Gaspar had been lost. The next year Miguel set out to find his brother, and from this voyage he failed to return. The two brave brothers, the first Europeans to explore our coasts since the time of the Vikings, were probably both shipwrecked and drowned. Exploration in small ships in unknown waters was very dangerous.

The Corte-Reals learned a great deal about the coasts of

Gaspar Corte-Real, whose statue stands today in St. John's, explored the East Coast of Newfoundland as far as Placentia Bay and gave many of the places there Portuguese names. On his second voyage he took one ship to make a voyage of exploration southward and was probably shipwrecked or lost at sea.

Newfoundland. They provided information which made possible the preparation of maps and charts. They also learned something of the native peoples of Newfoundland, because Gaspar on his second voyage sent back to Portugal fifty-seven Indians whom he had captured.

For many years the coasts of Newfoundland and Labrador were known as the "Land of Corte-Real". Even now, place names given by the Portuguese—names such as Cape Race, Cape Spear, Cape Bonavista, Baccalieu, Fermeuse, and many others—remind us that the Portuguese explored our shores. Also, of course, large numbers of hardy Portuguese fishermen still come each year to fish on the Grand Banks.

Explore and Discover

1. If you live in St. John's or visit St. John's, go to the Confederation Building and see the statue of Gaspar Corte-Real. Why do you think the statue shows Corte-Real looking towards the northwest?
2. With the help of a map, make a list of all the Portuguese place names on the East Coast of Newfoundland. Ask your teacher to help you.

7 Jacques Cartier

By this time a great deal of money had been spent and many brave men lost on voyages of exploration, but no gold, silver, jewels, or spices had been brought back to Europe. All attempts to find a passage to China and India by sailing to the northwest had been blocked by floating fields of ice.

There were some explorers, however, who still believed that such a passage could be found. One such man was Sebastian Cabot, the son of John Cabot. Another was Jacques Cartier, a French sailor from the port of St. Malo. Fishermen from this port of France were already familiar with the fishing grounds of Newfoundland. Cartier, who had been made "Captain and Pilot for the King", decided to try to succeed where the Cabots and the Corte-Reals had failed—in finding the Northwest Passage to Asia.

One morning in April, 1534, Cartier set sail from St. Malo with two small ships. Twenty days later he sighted Cape Bonavista and shortly afterwards entered a harbour which he named St. Catherine's Haven. This harbour we now call Catalina. Here his men rested and Cartier refitted his ships. He then sailed north along the coast of Newfoundland. When he reached the Strait of Belle Isle, he thought that he had perhaps found the passage to Asia. He sailed through the Strait, along the West Coast of Newfoundland, and then across the Gulf of St. Lawrence to what is now Prince Edward Island and

Cartier became a skilful sailor while making trading voyages to Portugal. On behalf of the King of France he later made three voyages in search of the Northwest Passage. On his third voyage he tried to establish a colony on the banks of the St. Lawrence but was not successful.

the coast of New Brunswick. From there, Cartier explored the Bay of Chaleur and the Gaspé Peninsula. He then returned to St. Malo by way of the north shore of the Gulf of St. Lawrence and the Strait of Belle Isle.

The following year Cartier returned. This time as he sailed north along the Newfoundland coast, he stopped at the Funk Islands, where his crew killed two boat-loads of Great Auks. Since the wings of this bird were very small, it was unable to fly, and in the early days fishermen killed it in great numbers for food and bait. In the end all the Great Auks were killed and today there are none left anywhere in the world.

From the Funks, Cartier again sailed north and entered the Gulf of St. Lawrence through the Strait of Belle Isle. This time he sailed up the St. Lawrence until rapids in the river stopped his progress near the place where the city of Montreal now stands. Before he could return to the open sea, the river had frozen, and he was forced to spend the winter near the site of the present city of Quebec.

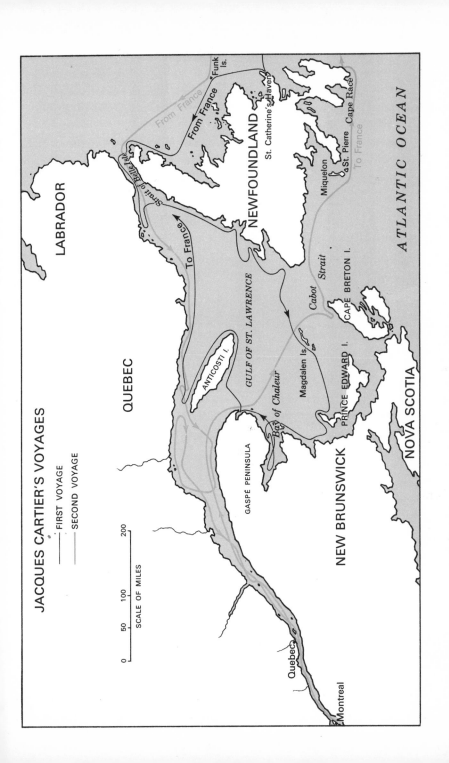

JACQUES CARTIER'S VOYAGES

——— FIRST VOYAGE
——— SECOND VOYAGE

SCALE OF MILES

0   50   100   200

LABRADOR

QUEBEC

NEWFOUNDLAND

St. Catherine's Haven

Funk Is.

From France

From France

Strait of Belle Isle

To France

To France

Cape Race

St. Pierre

Miquelon

ATLANTIC OCEAN

Cabot Strait

CAPE BRETON I.

GULF OF ST. LAWRENCE

ANTICOSTI I.

Magdalen Is.

PRINCE EDWARD I.

Bay of Chaleur

GASPÉ PENINSULA

NEW BRUNSWICK

NOVA SCOTIA

Quebec

Montreal

In the spring Cartier sailed down the river, through the Cabot Strait, and along the South Coast of Newfoundland, and so returned home to St. Malo.

Cartier had made two great discoveries. He had not found the Northwest Passage to Asia, but he had discovered and explored the great St. Lawrence River and the mainland of Canada. He had also sailed through both the Strait of Belle Isle and the Cabot Strait, thus proving that Newfoundland was an island.

Explore and Discover

1. What is the Northwest Passage? Why were explorers very anxious to find it? Why were they not successful?
2. How did Cartier prove that Newfoundland was an island? What was the other discovery that he made?
3. Read about a visit to the Funk Islands in a book called *The Secret Islands* by Franklin Russell.

8 Fishermen Come from Europe

While explorers were busy mapping the coasts of Newfoundland and Labrador and looking for the Northwest Passage, fishermen from England, France, Spain, and Portugal came every year to fish in Newfoundland waters and to dry their fish on the island's shores.

In the early days the French and Portuguese fishermen were the most active. There were several reasons why this was so. Both countries had long, hot summers when a great amount of salt could be made from sea-water to preserve fish. Both had large Roman Catholic populations who ate fish rather than meat on many days throughout the year. Both countries needed large quantities of dried fish to supply to their armies and navies.

Then came the Spanish and the English fishermen. But the English were not so fortunate as the others, for the climate of England was not hot enough for the making of salt. To overcome this difficulty, they reached an agreement with the Portuguese, who had plenty of salt to sell. English and Portuguese fishermen therefore fished in the same areas.

During the first one hundred years after Cabot's voyage, fishermen from many countries came to the shores of Newfoundland. The English and Portuguese fished mainly along the shores of the Avalon Peninsula. The French fished further to the north as well as along the South and West Coasts.

This drawing from Molls Map of 1712-14 shows an early fishing room. When the fish was cured and dried, it was piled in great stacks and covered with brush until the time came for it to be taken to the countries of Europe.

Spanish fishermen, and French too, fished far out to sea on the Grand Banks. And fishermen of all nations often visited the Funk Islands to kill Great Auks, which were their principal source of fresh meat.

Newfoundland was now a busy place during the summertime, when hundreds of ships and thousands of men filled the harbours. But when autumn came, they all sailed away to return to their homes in England, France, Spain, and Portugal. Some ships, however, left a few men behind to protect their stages and flakes during the winter and to prepare for the return of the ships in the spring. The winters must have been lonely for these men, who were the first settlers on our island.

Explore and Discover

1. Why did ships of many nations come to Newfoundland each year?
2. Draw or trace a map of Newfoundland and the Grand Banks.
3. Try to find out the names of all the different nations that send ships to fish on the Grand Banks of Newfoundland today.
4. Why did the English and the Portuguese fishermen fish near each other?
5. With the help of your teacher, find out how salt for the curing of fish was made from sea-water and write down what you learn.
6. Who were the first settlers in Newfoundland?

9 Newfoundland Is Claimed for England

At this time many people in England thought of starting colonies and bringing people to live in the New World. One such man was Sir Humphrey Gilbert, who received permission from Queen Elizabeth to start a colony in North America.

In 1583 he set sail from England with five ships. After he had crossed the Atlantic, he found that he was short of supplies and decided to stop at St. John's to collect some.

Gilbert found thirty-six ships in St. John's, of which twenty were Spanish and Portuguese. He persuaded the captains of these ships to give him food supplies, including wine, marmalade, biscuits, and sweet oil.

When he had obtained his provisions, Gilbert decided to claim Newfoundland for England. He therefore assembled all the fishermen in the port, read to them his orders from the Queen, and declared that from that time on, all the land for six hundred miles round belonged to England.

Shortly afterwards Gilbert set sail for the mainland. He left no settlers behind, nor did he leave anyone to govern the land which he had claimed for Queen Elizabeth.

In fact, Gilbert was not a successful colonizer. His expedition had been badly prepared. He was short of supplies. Many of his crew were rowdies and criminals who had been taken

In 1576 Gilbert wrote a book on the Northwest Passage. Later he was granted a charter of exploration. After he was lost, the charter was given to his half-brother, Sir Walter Raleigh, by Elizabeth I.

from jails in England. One of his five ships had had to return to England with sick crew members even before it reached Newfoundland. Another became a pirate ship, and a third was wrecked on Sable Island. With only two small ships remaining, Gilbert decided to return to England. On the way back the smaller of the two, the *Squirrel*, a little vessel of only ten tons in which Gilbert himself sailed, was lost at sea. The other, the *Golden Hind*, reached England safely. Luckily, the captain of the *Golden Hind* had kept a diary in which we find the story of this unfortunate expedition.

You will remember that several years before Cabot's voyage, Spain and Portugal, with the consent of the Pope, had divided the undiscovered part of the world between them.

35

Newfoundland had been part of the Spanish share. By claiming Newfoundland for England, Gilbert had now challenged the Spanish claim.

Even though Sir Humphrey Gilbert did not start a settlement in Newfoundland, his voyage was still very important, because the King of Spain saw that England was no longer going to pay attention to his claim that he owned Newfoundland. To make certain that he understood this, Queen Elizabeth sent a fleet of ships under the command of Sir Bernard Drake to attack Spanish fishermen in Newfoundland. In 1585 Drake arrived off the Newfoundland coast and destroyed most of the Spanish fleet. From this time on, the English fishermen had the East Coast of Newfoundland to themselves. The French still fished on the South and West Coasts.

Explore and Discover

1. As a class project, make a newspaper for the day August 5, 1583. First write stories for your newspaper. One story might tell how Gilbert claimed Newfoundland for England and why this was an important event. Other stories might tell about the troubles the ships had while crossing the Atlantic. Then make drawings for your newspaper. Draw the harbour and the many fishing ships in it, Gilbert's ships, and Gilbert's claiming of Newfoundland. Write any other stories and make any other drawings that you like.

2. After Gilbert claimed Newfoundland for England, how did the English show the Spaniards that they meant to keep Newfoundland as an English colony?

10   Fishermen and Settlers

In the West Country of England there were many merchants and shipowners who thought they could make good profits by sending fishing ships to Newfoundland. We now call these men the "Western Adventurers". Each year they sent out more than one hundred ships to Newfoundland. The ships arrived in June and began fishing as soon as weather and ice conditions would allow. They built stages, wharves, flakes, and stores. In autumn, when the fish had been dried, they loaded it into their ships and carried it back across the ocean to sell in England, France, Spain, and Portugal. Some ships came not to catch fish but to buy it from the fishermen. These ships sometimes took their fish to Spain to trade for cargoes of wine. This wine was called "sack", and the ships that carried it were called "sack" ships.

Many people in England thought that the fishermen would catch more fish if they lived in Newfoundland all the year round. By doing so, they would be able to build their boats and stages and flakes, cut their firewood, and prepare their fishing equipment during the winter. They would then be ready to begin fishing very early in the spring and, if they did not have to return to England in the fall, could continue fishing much longer each year. Also, if there were settlers in Newfoundland throughout the year, they would be able to prevent French, Spanish, and Portuguese fishermen from fishing in Newfound-

This modern-day photograph shows cod being dried in Petty Harbour. Flakes and stages such as these have been built in Newfoundland for four and a half centuries. The Grand Banks, a part of the continental shelf off the coast of Newfoundland, are among the largest fishing grounds in the world.

land waters. Thus English fishermen would control the whole Newfoundland fishery.

But the Western Adventurers had several reasons for not wanting settlers in Newfoundland. They knew that settlers would take the best fishing places, the best harbours, and the best sites for flakes and stages. They believed, too, that if many people came to live in Newfoundland, they would begin to build their own boats and to make their own ropes, nets, hooks, lines, anchors, and other things needed for the fishery. In this way many workers in England would lose their jobs. They also thought that the settlers would begin to grow their own vegetables and raise their own cattle and feared that farmers in England, who raised food for the fishing fleet, would suffer. For all these reasons, the Western Adventurers decided to try to prevent anyone from living in Newfoundland.

Both the people who wished to settle in Newfoundland and those who wanted to prevent people from settling here went to King Charles I to ask for his support. The King wished to please both groups. He therefore gave permission to a group of merchants from London and Bristol to start a colony in Newfoundland. At the same time, he ordered them not to interfere with the fishermen who came in the summer.

Explore and Discover

1. Who were the Western Adventurers? Why did they want to send fishing ships to Newfoundland?

2. Discuss with your teacher why people in England wanted only English ships to fish in Newfoundland.

3. Divide your class into two groups. Let one group be the Western Adventurers and the other group be those who wished to settle in Newfoundland. Ask your teacher to play the part of King Charles I. Each side should prepare its arguments for and against settlement. After all have helped to prepare the arguments for their side, perhaps one person from each side can be chosen to present them to the King.

4. Do you think the King's decision was a good one? Why?

11 John Guy's Settlement

The London and Bristol merchants chose a man named John Guy to lead the settlers to Newfoundland.

The King had granted the colonists all the land between Cape St. Mary's and Cape Bonavista. Guy chose Cupids as the site of his settlement. Here he built a large house, which he called "Sea Forest Plantation". He also built wharves, stores, stages, houses for the settlers, and a fort for protection. Soon land was cleared for a farm. Sheep, goats, pigs, cows, and hens had been brought to Newfoundland, and crops were planted. Some of the settlers engaged in fishing.

John Guy had made a good beginning, but the West Country fishermen were determined to destroy his colony. He made laws to protect the colonists and their property and to preserve the forests and fishing grounds. But the fishermen would not obey his laws. They said that the King had ordered Guy not to interfere with them.

Moreover, Guy's colony was raided by pirates. Many pirate ships cruised round the coast of Newfoundland. They seized fishing ships and sack ships. They destroyed settlements and carried off large numbers of fishermen. They also stole boats, arms and ammunition, food and provisions, as well as cargoes of dried fish and wine. One year Guy claimed that pirates had stolen goods worth £20,000 from his colony.

Pirates often chose their captains by vote and drew up their own rules called "pirate articles". Some of them tried to set up colonies of their own where they kept their goods and money in a common hiding-place.

The most famous of all the pirates who operated in Newfoundland waters was Peter Easton. His headquarters were at Ferryland. Another well-known pirate who spent one summer in Newfoundland was Sir Henry Mainwaring. But the most dangerous of all were the Sallee Rovers, so named because they sailed from the harbour of Sallee in North Africa. They became so powerful that the English government was finally forced to send a fleet to Sallee to try to destroy them. But it was not until much later, after the United States had become independent and had sent ships to fight them, that the Sallee Rovers ceased to be a danger to shipping.

John Guy stayed in Newfoundland for only two years. The merchants then sent Captain John Mason to govern the colony. But the West Country fishermen, the pirates, the cold weather, and the rocky soil discouraged the colonists, and there were too few colonists to make profits. Finally, the London and Bristol Company saw that it was not going to get anything in return for the large amount of money it had spent on the colony. The merchants then decided to sell some of their land.

Explore and Discover

1. Make a list of all the things John Guy's settlers would have to do to establish their colony.
2. What do you think would be the greatest hardships that the new settlers would have to face?
3. Why do you think the West Country fishermen wanted to destroy Guy's colony?
4. With the help of your teacher, find some pirate stories to read. How did pirates make a living?
5. Draw a picture of a pirate ship.
6. Why do you think Guy could not defend his colony against pirates?
7. Why did the London and Bristol merchants decide to sell some of their land?

12   Other Settlements

There were many men in England who wanted land in the New World. Some men believed that they would make a fortune if they owned a colony. Some wanted to live in a place where they could practise their own religion without fear. Others believed that colonies would be good places to send criminals.

Thus the London and Bristol Company had no trouble selling land. It sold some to Sir William Vaughan, some to Lord Falkland, and some to Lord Baltimore.

Sir William Vaughan sent colonists to Trepassey, but he himself stayed at home in Wales. Colonists in Newfoundland had to work very hard at cutting trees, clearing land, and fishing. They had to build houses, stores, stages, and wharves and grow vegetables. Vaughan's colonists did not work hard: they did not even build houses but lived in fishermen's stages. For this reason the colony was a failure.

Lord Falkland also failed to start a successful colony. Like Sir William Vaughan, he did not know how difficult life in a new land could be. He also sent men who were not willing to work hard to make new homes in the wilderness.

Lord Baltimore was a little more successful. He was a Roman Catholic who wanted to build a home where he could practise his religion freely. He settled at Ferryland and built a very fine stone house which he called the "Mansion House".

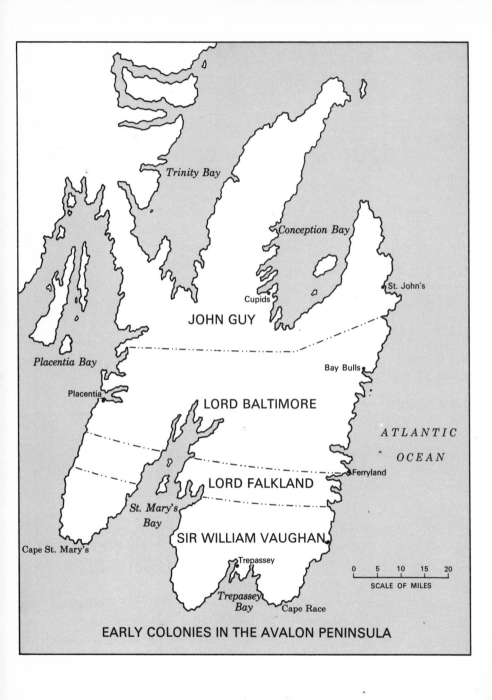

Trinity Bay

Conception Bay

St. John's

Cupids

JOHN GUY

Placentia Bay

Bay Bulls

Placentia

LORD BALTIMORE

ATLANTIC

OCEAN

Ferryland

LORD FALKLAND

St. Mary's
Bay

SIR WILLIAM VAUGHAN

Cape St. Mary's

0   5   10   15   20

SCALE OF MILES

Trepassey

Trepassey
Bay   Cape Race

EARLY COLONIES IN THE AVALON PENINSULA

He brought cattle to his colony, planted gardens, and engaged in fishing. But he also had difficulties. Many of his colonists became ill because they did not have enough fresh food. The soil was rocky and hard to cultivate. Pirates and French warships attacked his ships as well as the colony. Moreover, the winters at Ferryland were colder than winters in England. Lady Baltimore found them particularly hard to bear. Finally, after nearly ten years, Baltimore decided to leave Newfoundland for a warmer climate. He went on to found a colony that was to become the state of Maryland in the United States of America. In that state the great city of Baltimore is named for him.

Explore and Discover

1. Find three reasons why people in England wanted to buy land in Newfoundland. Perhaps your teacher can help you to think of other reasons as well.
2. Why did the colonies established by Sir William Vaughan and Lord Falkland fail?
3. Why did Lord Baltimore come to Newfoundland?
4. Make a plan of what the colony at Ferryland might have included. Your plan should show places for the houses, stores, and stages of the settlers, as well as gardens for growing vegetables and fishing boats in the harbour. Show Mansion House also.
5. What three groups of people made life difficult for the settlers?
6. Imagine that you were Lord Baltimore and write a letter to a friend in England telling why, after ten years in Newfoundland, you have decided to move to Maryland.

13   The First Western Charter

Even though the colonies established by Guy, Baltimore, Vaughan, and Falkland had all failed, some of the settlers had remained in Newfoundland. Other settlers, too, had come to the island to stay. They were fishermen who wanted to remain in Newfoundland during the winter to cut wood and build wharves, stages, and houses so that they would be ready for fishing very early in the spring. After a while many of them came to like the new land and to think of it as home.

But most West Country shipowners and merchants were alarmed when they thought of settlement. They feared that settlers would come to every harbour and take the best places for fishing rooms, as well as the best fishing grounds. They also feared that settlers would be able to sell fish to Spain, Portugal, France, and Italy more cheaply than they could. Also, the settlers might not buy provisions from the West Country merchants.

Thus the merchants decided to ask the King to give them control of Newfoundland. They told the King that if he wished to be a powerful monarch, he should have a strong navy and train many sailors. The best way to train sailors, the merchants said, was to send them to Newfoundland every summer as fishermen. In this way they would become used to large ships and sailing on the open ocean.

Fishing admirals could usually be bribed with money, food, or a glass of rum. They had the power to punish men as harshly as they pleased.

The King and the men who advised him, who were known as his Privy Council, liked the idea of England's becoming a powerful nation. They agreed to do as the Western Adventurers asked, hoping that if they carried out this plan, they would have a strong navy. Thus in 1634 King Charles I issued the First Western Charter.

The purpose of the charter was to discourage settlers and to make the entire coast of Newfoundland available to visiting fishing ships from England. The most important part of the First Western Charter gave rules to control the fishermen during the fishing season. It established the rule of the fishing admirals.

Under this rule the captain of the first fishing vessel to arrive in any harbour in the spring became admiral of the harbour for that year. The second arrival became vice-admiral, and the third arrival became rear admiral. These men could take all the best fishing premises for their own use and could enforce the laws listed in the charter. They could take criminals back to England for punishment. If any settlers happened to live in their harbour, the fishing admirals could chase them away or treat them as badly as they wished.

The First Western Charter made it very hard for settlers to live in Newfoundland. It did not matter who had built the houses, stages, wharves, and stores in the harbours and coves along the coast. When a fishing admiral arrived, he would take what he wanted and give the rest to his friends. In any case, the West Country shipowners did not like settlers, and we can well imagine that the fishing admirals would not be very kind to them.

Explore and Discover

1. Imagine that you were a Western Adventurer and write a letter to King Charles I telling why you should be allowed to keep colonists out of Newfoundland.
2. What argument persuaded the King to issue the First Western Charter?
3. What was the First Western Charter meant to achieve?
4. Who were the fishing admirals?
5. Why do you think fishing admirals might be bad rulers?

14   Sir David Kirke

It seemed that the First Western Charter had decided the fate of settlers in Newfoundland forever. But the King had other friends besides the Western Adventurers. Some of these men now came forward to ask that Sir David Kirke be allowed to start a colony in Newfoundland.

Kirke was a brave and adventurous man. Some years earlier, when England and France had been at war, he had captured the city of Quebec from the French. At the time of the capture the two countries had already made peace, but Kirke had not known this because in those days it took news a long time to travel across the Atlantic Ocean. When the news had arrived, he had had no choice but to give Quebec back to the French governor.

The King knew that Kirke was disappointed because he had been forced to return Quebec to the French. He agreed to reward Kirke now by allowing him to set up a colony in Newfoundland. Kirke was named governor of all Newfoundland and was given the coat of arms that is still used by the Province of Newfoundland and Labrador today.

The King knew that his grant to Kirke would anger the Western Adventurers. In order that they might be less angry, he gave Kirke a charter stating that none of the settlers should live within six miles of the sea-shore and that none of them should take part in the fishery.

The Coat of Arms of Newfoundland was granted to Sir David Kirke on January 1, 1637. The two lions and two unicorns in the centre are separated by the Cross of St. George, representing Newfoundland's ties with Great Britain. The caribou and the Indians represent Newfoundland.

However, Kirke knew that settlers in Newfoundland could not make a living if they could not fish. He also knew that the First Western Charter had said that all subjects of the King should be free to fish anywhere in Newfoundland. He therefore decided that he would obey only those parts of his own charter which pleased him. When he came to Newfoundland, he moved into Baltimore's Mansion House at Ferryland. He built forts at Ferryland, Bay Bulls, and St. John's. The settlers whom he brought also settled by the sea.

Very soon Kirke was governing a growing settlement. He sold fishing licences and rented fishing premises. He also sold licences to tavern keepers. He made all foreign fishermen pay him a tax of five fish for every one hundred and twenty they caught. He brought many fishermen out from England and paid them wages to catch fish for him. He worked hard to establish a prosperous colony at Ferryland.

It seemed that at last Newfoundland was to be properly colonized and properly governed. Then certain events occurred in England which changed everything. The English Parliament believed that it, not the King, should rule the country. The supporters of Parliament, led by Oliver Cromwell, therefore went to war against the King's followers, who were called Royalists. In the end Parliament won the war and King Charles was beheaded. The new government under Cromwell was very suspicious of all who had been Royalists.

Kirke had been a good friend of King Charles. West Country shipowners and merchants, who hated Kirke because his colony was successful, now went to Cromwell and said that Kirke was a Royalist. They also claimed that Kirke was collecting a fleet at Ferryland which would be used to chase Cromwell out of England and put a king back on the throne.

These stories were not true, but Cromwell decided to bring Kirke back to England for trial and to send his own men to Newfoundland to manage the colony. The trial proved that the charges against Kirke were false. Before he could get back to Newfoundland, however, he was again arrested. This time Lord Baltimore charged that Kirke had taken his house at Ferryland without permission. Before the new trial could be held, Kirke died in the Clink Prison.

So ended the last attempt to develop a properly governed English colony in Newfoundland. Sir David Kirke had been a strong and intelligent man. Despite the West Country fishermen he had built a prosperous community at Ferryland. He might have given Newfoundland a strong government in its early days, but the war in England had interfered and his death brought an end to the plans he had made. Hardy fishermen continued to make Newfoundland their home, but for a long time they had no government except the cruel fishing admirals.

Explore and Discover

1. Why was Sir David Kirke allowed to start a colony in Newfoundland?
2. Before Kirke was named governor for all Newfoundland, who were the only rulers that the settlers in Newfoundland had?
3. What order in the First Western Charter was different from the order in Kirke's charter that no settlers should take part in the fishery?
4. Why did the settlers have to live near the sea?
5. Why do you think Kirke built forts at Ferryland, Bay Bulls, and St. John's?
6. Make a list of the things Kirke did to establish a good colony at Ferryland.
7. Who were Kirke's enemies in England? Why were they angry at him?
8. Who were the Royalists? Why was Kirke thought to be a Royalist?
9. Explain how the quarrel between the King and the Parliament in England ruined Kirke's colony.

15 King William's Act

All the colonies in Newfoundland had now been destroyed. The Government of England said that Newfoundland could not be a colony, but only a place where English fishermen could work during the summer months. The fish they caught would be sold to Spain and Portugal, and the money they earned would be taken home to make England richer. Therefore, every spring a fishing fleet from England crossed the Atlantic Ocean to Newfoundland and every autumn it returned.

Of course, there were many settlers living in Newfoundland throughout the year. The Government of England, however, pretended that they were not there. Britain did not think it necessary to build roads, schools, or churches, nor did she provide laws and a government. She simply pretended that Newfoundland disappeared when the last fishing ship left it for England in the autumn.

But the West Country fishermen who came each year to fish saw that the number of settlers was growing and that homes were being built in nearly every good fishing harbour between Cape Race and Cape Bonavista. They knew that the English government's pretence would not drive the settlers away, nor prevent others from coming. So once again they went to the King to seek his help.

The new King, Charles II, remembered that his father had been beheaded because he had angered the merchants of Eng-

Charles II favoured the Western Adventurers. He renewed the First Western Charter and did not put a tax on the fish that the West Country fishermen caught. He refused to appoint a governor for Newfoundland.

land and their supporters in Parliament. He was afraid to oppose their wishes. He therefore ordered that the First Western Charter should be obeyed and that fishing ships should not take anyone to Newfoundland who wanted to fish from the shore.

Still the Western Adventurers were not satisfied. They wanted all settlement in Newfoundland destroyed. Once again the King agreed to do as they wished. He commanded the naval officers who were sent out each year to protect English fishermen in Newfoundland to move all Newfoundlanders back to England or to make them go to the West Indies.

Commodore Sir John Berry was given those orders in 1675. He sailed along the coast of Newfoundland, counting all the settlers and talking to them. He learned that they did not wish to leave their homes. He knew that they had no money with which to pay passage to England or to the West Indies. He believed that it would be very cruel to force them to move. Therefore, he reported to the Government of England that the plan was impossible.

The government was not as sympathetic towards the settlers as Sir John Berry was, but it accepted his report. It agreed to let Newfoundlanders remain in Newfoundland. However, it also agreed to let the fishing admirals deal with them in any way they liked. For the next two years the fishing admirals undertook to tear down every house between Cape Race and Cape Bonavista. The settlers suffered greatly, but there was nothing they could do except try to build new homes, perhaps in harbours where the fishing admirals would not bother them.

Both the fishing admirals and the English government finally realized that Newfoundlanders were not going to be driven from their homes. In 1699 the English Parliament passed the First Newfoundland Act, which we call King William's Act. This act said that fishing admirals would continue to rule New-foundland, but it also contained two rules which were very important to the settlers. It said that if a settler had built fish-ing premises which had not been used by English ships during the past fifteen years, he owned these premises and they could not be seized by a West Country fisherman. Secondly, it said that if a settler or fisherman did not agree with a rule made by the fishing admirals, he could complain to the captain of any British warship in Newfoundland. The settlers believed that naval officers would act more fairly than fishing admirals.

Explore and Discover

1. Discuss with your teacher why the English government ignored the settlers in Newfoundland.
2. Why did the Western Adventurers ask King Charles II for help?
3. What orders did Charles II give to help the Western Adventurers? Why did he favour them?
4. Imagine that you were Sir John Berry and write a report to Charles II telling why you believe that the order to move all the settlers from Newfoundland is not a good one.
5. How did the fishing admirals try to drive the settlers away?
6. In what ways did King William's Act help the settlers?

16   The French

While the English government was trying to destroy all settlements in Newfoundland, the French government was doing the very opposite. France, too, believed that the Newfoundland fisheries were very important because they were a source of food and money for France and also because fishermen who had worked on the Grand Banks made good sailors for the French navy. But the King of France thought that the best way to control the fisheries was to have a colony in Newfoundland.

Ever since the discovery of Newfoundland, the French had been sending out fishing fleets each year. They had fished from the South Coast and from the Great Northern Peninsula, while the English had worked on the East Coast. About the same time that King Charles II agreed to move all English settlers from Newfoundland, King Louis of France ordered that a French colony should be established at Plaisance, which we now call Placentia.

Soon settlers were brought from France. Forts to protect the harbour were built. Houses, stores, and wharves were constructed. Flakes were unnecessary because Plaisance had a very large beach upon which fish could be dried. As Plaisance became a prosperous little town, French settlers moved out to inhabit other harbours and islands in Placentia Bay and along the South Coast.

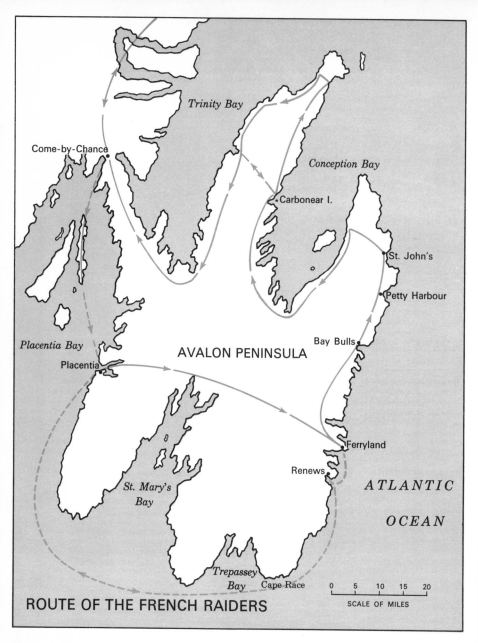

ROUTE OF THE FRENCH RAIDERS

Note the solid line showing the land route of the French raiders. The broken line from Plaisance to Ferryland shows the warships' sea route.

D'Iberville was born in Montreal and sailed on his father's trading ship on the St. Lawrence when he was fourteen. Later he fought against the English in North America and in the Caribbean. In 1703 he was appointed governor of Louisiana, which was at that time a French colony.

At this time Canada was a French colony and King Louis thought that Newfoundland should be part of Canada, that is, that Newfoundland, too, should belong to France. For thirty years after the settlement of Plaisance, the French and English lived peacefully side by side. Then war broke out between England and France. The governor of Canada and the governor of Plaisance at once decided that they would attack and destroy all English settlements in Newfoundland.

The French planned to attack the East Coast settlements by sea and by land. The governor of Plaisance, De Brouillan, sailed his ships to Renews, while the land attack was led by a very brave and successful French Canadian soldier and woodsman named D'Iberville. D'Iberville had come from Quebec with soldiers, woodsmen, and Indians, leading them from Plaisance across half-frozen rivers and bogs through trackless woods to Ferryland.

At Ferryland, D'Iberville was joined by De Brouillan and together, leading their soldiers and Indians, they marched towards St. John's. At Petty Harbour the English settlers tried to stop the French attack, but thirty-six of them were killed and the rest fled to St. John's. Another battle was fought near Bay Bulls, and here fifty-five settlers were killed. One hundred others escaped in a ship. The French marched on to St. John's, where all the settlers were sheltered in a fort. The fort held out for three days, but when D'Iberville threatened to send in his Indians with their scalping knives, it surrendered.

Three hundred men, women, and children were crowded into ships and sent off to England. All the buildings in St. John's, except two or three houses which were used as hospitals, were burned after everything of value had been taken by D'Iberville's men.

De Brouillan and the soldiers now sailed back to Plaisance, while D'Iberville with his Canadians and Indians set out to march round Conception Bay and Trinity Bay, attacking, looting, and destroying every settlement on the way. Three hundred settlers, however, escaped to Carbonear Island, where they successfully defended themselves against attack. At Bonavista, too, a brave New Englander named Michael Gill led the settlers in a successful defence of their homes. D'Iberville, with seven hundred prisoners and the loot from the English settlements, now marched across the Isthmus of Avalon to a point near the present settlement of Come-by-Chance and from there sailed back to Plaisance.

The poor settlers who remained in Newfoundland must have suffered greatly that winter. Their homes had been burned, and everything of value had been looted and carried to Plaisance. But many of them survived. Most of the seven hundred prisoners who had been taken to Plaisance escaped and returned to their homes. Soon the settlements were rebuilt and St. John's was provided with a new fort and a garrison of soldiers.

During the next eight years the settlers were left in peace to rebuild their homes. English naval ships during these years

Before the French signed the Treaty of Utrecht in 1713, they tried several times to take over Newfoundland. D'Iberville led the first attack in 1696. Other attacks were made in 1705 and 1709. The attacks were supported by French warships, but the main force of raiders marched from Plaisance because the English settlements were difficult to defend from the land side.

destroyed French fishing ships and rooms at Trepassey, St. Mary's, Colinet, St. Lawrence, and St. Pierre, but they did not dare attack the well-fortified harbour of Plaisance. Then in 1705 the governor of Plaisance, De Subercase, decided to launch another attack upon the East Coast settlements.

Early in January on a Sunday morning, De Subercase, with four hundred and fifty soldiers and several hundred settlers from Plaisance—Canadians and Micmac Indians—surprised the sleeping town of St. John's. Over three hundred settlers were herded into a church, where they were held prisoner.

But the garrison of about eighty men defended themselves in the fort. For thirty-three days the fort held out, and finally the French were forced to leave without having captured it. Once again the town was plundered and burned. Eighty of the male prisoners from the church were forced to carry the loot back to Plaisance.

From St. John's part of the French force, including the Micmacs, set out to plunder the settlements around Conception, Trinity, and Bonavista Bays. Again Carbonear Island proved to be a safe refuge, but every other settlement was destroyed. This time the man who was in command at Bonavista, George Skeffington, surrendered the town without a fight and paid £450 in ransom for his own life.

The French claimed that all English settlement in Newfoundland had been destroyed, but the settlers refused to admit defeat. Once again they began the difficult task of rebuilding what had been destroyed.

The citizens of St. John's had only four years of peace. Then, on a January morning two hours before dawn, the French attacked again. There were now three forts in St. John's, but the gates of two were open and the third surrendered. This time the settlers paid a ransom of over £7,000 worth of fish for the town. The officers of the garrison were sent to France, and one hundred and fifty prisoners were taken to Plaisance and forced to work for the French.

Four years later the war ended. Though the French had been victorious in Newfoundland, they had been defeated in Europe. The Treaty of Utrecht, which set forth the terms of peace, declared that from now on all Newfoundland was British territory. The French were ordered to leave Plaisance and were forbidden ever to start another colony in Newfoundland. However, they were given permission to come every summer to fish in Newfoundland waters and to land and dry their fish along the shore between Cape Bonavista and Point Riche.

Explore and Discover

1. How were French settlers in Newfoundland treated differently from English settlers?
2. Find two reasons why the French decided to attack the English settlements in Newfoundland.
3. Why did St. John's surrender to D'Iberville?
4. Imagine that you were living in St. John's at the time of D'Iberville's attack and write a story telling what happened.
5. Why did ships of the Royal Navy not attack Plaisance?
6. Imagine that you were a soldier in De Subercase's force and write a letter to your family in France telling about your adventures.
7. Explain why the French had to leave the colony at Plaisance. What were they still allowed to do?

17 The Naval Governors

In the years following the end of the French wars, the population of Newfoundland slowly increased. Still the settlers were given no courts of law to protect them, nor any government to assist them. Newfoundland had neither roads nor schools nor any kind of public building. The fishing admirals, supervised by the commodore of the naval convoy, ruled during the summer months, but in winter the island was lawless.

The settlers were at the mercy of the merchants and traders and were often badly treated. Sometimes traders would force fishermen to buy large quantities of rum or other expensive goods before selling the fishermen the salt that they needed to cure fish. Fishermen were rarely given money for their fish but had to take trade goods in return. Most fishermen were in debt, and sometimes traders seized all their boats and property as payment, thus making it impossible for the fishermen to earn a living. Many fishermen escaped each year to New England, and many sold themselves as indentured servants to American traders.

Not all settlers were poor. Some had become quite prosperous. In St. John's, Harbour Grace, Carbonear, Trinity, and other settlements there were well-to-do boat owners and merchants who lived in fine houses and enjoyed many luxuries. But most fishermen and servants lived in poverty.

The commodores knew that the fishing admirals usually favoured their friends and did not do their duty towards the settlers. They certainly knew that during the long winter months there was no government at all. For these reasons they suggested to the British government that the king should appoint a proper governor for Newfoundland.

Of course the Western Adventurers did not like this idea. They wanted to send all the settlers to Nova Scotia or some other colony. Neither the king nor Parliament agreed with them, however, partly because they knew that it would be difficult to force the stubborn Newfoundlanders to leave their homes, and partly because it would be very expensive. But for many years they paid no attention to the commodores' reports either.

At last in 1728, a very important man, Lord Vere Beauclerk, was made commodore. He told the British government that it could no longer ignore Newfoundland because there were many settlers on the island. He talked about the lawlessness during the winter months and claimed that Newfoundland should have a governor to prevent the settlers from being badly treated.

The British government soon announced that a governor would be appointed. He would have power to name justices of the peace and to establish court houses and prisons. However, in order not to offend the Western Adventurers, Britain said that the governor of Newfoundland would not be allowed to interfere with the fishing admirals. Moreover, the governor would stay in Newfoundland only during the fishing season.

The first man to be appointed governor was Captain Henry Osborne. He divided the island into six districts and named justices of the peace as well as constables. These men would continue to enforce the law during the winter months. The fishing admirals were very angry because they wanted to con-

Lord Rodney was one of the ablest of the early governors of Newfoundland. In enforcing justice, he treated both fishermen and merchants alike. At the same time he protested strongly to the British government that the lack of good courts in Newfoundland made keeping order there very difficult.

tinue to do as they liked. But as long as Governor Osborne and Lord Vere Beauclerk remained in Newfoundland, they supported the new justices.

Not all the later governors were as good as Osborne, nor were all the commodores as eager to help the settlers as was Lord Vere Beauclerk. Some of the governors, however, were very able men. There was Captain John Byng, for example, and also Captain George Bridges Rodney, who later became one of Britain's greatest admirals. Under men like these, the island was peaceful, the justices did their duty, and the merchants and fishing admirals did not harm the settlers.

Other governors were very careless and did not take their duties seriously. Some of them did not even bother to write reports each year to the British government. Moreover, during certain years when Britain was at war, the governors did not even visit Newfoundland.

Some governors were as cruel as the fishing admirals themselves. Governor Dorrill, for example, tried to prevent Roman Catholics from owning property in Newfoundland. He ordered many houses to be torn down or burned and tried to force all Irishmen who were Roman Catholics to return to Ireland. At this time many Roman Catholics refused to swear loyalty to King George because they believed that Prince Charles Edward, usually called Bonnie Prince Charlie, should be king. Some of the governors, such as Governor Dorrill, feared that the Irish in Newfoundland would join the French and try to take over Newfoundland.

Neither the rule of the fishing admirals, nor the French wars, nor the bad treatment of the Irish made the Newfoundlanders give up hope. They rebuilt their homes time and again after they had been destroyed, and all the time the settlers grew in numbers and in strength.

Explore and Discover

1. In what two ways did the King try to please the Western Adventurers when he appointed a governor for Newfoundland?

2. Discuss with your classmates and your teacher why an officer in the British navy might be a good governor and why he might be a bad governor. Then write down what you have learned.

3. As a class project write a play about Captain Henry Osborne. Ask your teacher to help you. Your play could show Captain Osborne appointing justices of the peace and constables and dividing the island into districts. Show Osborne arguing with the fishing admirals and talking to the settlers. Then choose people to take the parts of the characters and present your play.

18   The Seven Years' War

In 1756 war broke out again between Britain and France. The battlegrounds of this war were in Canada, in India, in Europe, and in Newfoundland. During the first six years of the war, Newfoundland heard only the echoes. In fact, it was a prosperous time. Because a great deal of fish was needed to feed the armies and navies of the warring countries, the price of Newfoundland fish rose. Wages were high. The British navy was so busy fighting that it did not have time to enforce the laws against settlement. Thus hundreds of settlers came to stay in Newfoundland. Moreover, many merchants decided to remain in Newfoundland because they feared to cross the ocean with valuable cargoes that might be sunk by warships.

At last the war neared its end. France and England met in Paris to discuss peace terms. The French had lost Canada and had been defeated in India and in Europe. The British government thought that this might be a good time to force the French to give up all their fishing rights in Newfoundland.

The French, however, decided to show Britain that they were determined to keep these rights. Thus in the early spring of 1762, a French fleet escaped the British navy in a thick fog and headed for Newfoundland. On June 24 the fleet reached Bay Bulls, and eight hundred soldiers marched on St. John's. St. John's, Trinity, and Carbonear Island were captured with-

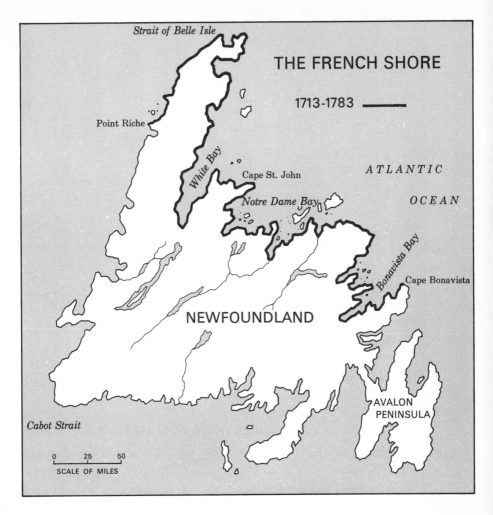

THE FRENCH SHORE

1713-1783 ——————

Strait of Belle Isle

Point Riche

White Bay

Cape St. John

Notre Dame Bay

ATLANTIC

OCEAN

Bonavista Bay

Cape Bonavista

NEWFOUNDLAND

AVALON
PENINSULA

Cabot Strait

0   25   50
SCALE OF MILES

out a fight. Now the French force set about repairing the forts in St. John's and building new defences on Signal Hill. Once more Newfoundland was under French control.

Lord Graves, the new governor of Newfoundland, was on his way from England when this happened. His ship was met on the Grand Banks and he was given the news. He ordered a party of Marines to head for Ferryland. He himself went to

Signal Hill overlooks the entrance to St. John's harbour. Thus it has always been an important point of defence. It is also well known because Marconi sent the first wireless message across the Atlantic from Cabot Tower. Today Signal Hill is a historic park that attracts many visitors.

Placentia and began to prepare its defences. Meanwhile, he had sent to the British forces in New York and Louisbourg for assistance.

Throughout the summer the French held St. John's. Then on September 11 a British force under the command of Colonel Amherst arrived off the Narrows of St. John's and prepared for an attack. The force landed at Torbay despite French opposition and marched towards St. John's. At Quidi Vidi another brief engagement was fought, but the French retreated towards Signal Hill. The next morning the Hill was assaulted and taken. The French fleet slipped its moorings and escaped in a fog, leaving the troops to their fate. The troops surrendered on September 20. This was the last battle fought between French and British troops during the conquest of North America by the British.

While all this had been happening, peace negotiations had been going on in Paris. The French had proved that they were willing to fight to keep a share in the Newfoundland fisheries and the British government, who did not wish to fight any longer, agreed to give them fishing rights. By the Treaty of Paris, the French were allowed to continue fishing and drying their fish on the coast of Newfoundland between Cape Bonavista and Point Riche. Also, the islands of St. Pierre and Miquelon were given to France to serve as shelters for French fishermen.

Explore and Discover

1. Why did settlement grow during the Seven Years' War?
2. Why did the French attack St. John's in 1762?
3. Why were the French allowed to keep the French Shore?
4. Draw or trace a map of Newfoundland. Colour Newfoundland one colour and colour the French Shore and the islands of St. Pierre and Miquelon differently to show that they were granted to France.
5. If you live in St. John's or visit St. John's, go to the Naval and Military Museum in the Confederation Building. Look at the model of Signal Hill and of the forts that were built in St. John's. Visit Signal Hill, too.
6. With the help of your teacher, learn as much as you can about the importance of Signal Hill in Newfoundland's history, and then write a few paragraphs telling what you have learned.

71

19   Sir Hugh Palliser

After the war the British government began the task of setting up governments in the territories it had conquered. Once again Newfoundland was treated differently from any other part of the British Empire. It was still not to be recognized as a colony. The coast of Labrador was added to the territory of Newfoundland, but settlement on that coast was forbidden. In fact, Labrador was added to Newfoundland in the hope that settlers could be kept away so that fishermen from the West Country would have more fishing grounds to themselves.

The British government was alarmed because settlement had grown so greatly during the war and decided to make one more attempt to crush it. For this task it appointed as governor of Newfoundland Sir Hugh Palliser, a very able naval officer. Palliser believed that the Newfoundland fisheries should be used to train sailors for the Royal Navy. Therefore he thought that the fisheries should be controlled by ships from England, not by settlers in Newfoundland.

Palliser tried very hard to enforce King William's Act. He wanted to keep more settlers from coming to Newfoundland and also to remove all settlement from Labrador. For this reason he tried to prevent smuggling and did not allow French fishermen to cut trees, build boats, or fish in the rivers for salmon. He hoped to keep the Eskimos in Labrador from hindering fishing ships and therefore encouraged the Moravian

As settlers and fishermen came to Newfoundland, the Beothucks
moved inland. When Palliser tried to befriend the tribe, many of
them had already been killed by the settlers and the Micmac Indians.

missionaries to begin their work on the northern Labrador
coast. For four years he worked very hard to give control of
the coast of Newfoundland and Labrador to English fishermen.

Palliser was hated by many settlers, by the traders, and by
the French, although he was doing only what he thought was
right. Since settlement was illegal, he claimed that the settlers
were breaking the law. Today we would perhaps disagree with
him because he thought that the law was a good one.

Although Palliser was cruel to settlers who, he thought, were
law-breakers, he should be remembered kindly for his attempt
to befriend the Beothucks. The Indians had been hunted like

Sir Hugh Palliser governed Newfoundland from 1764 to 1769. He did everything possible to prevent settlement in Newfoundland, but he encouraged exploration of the island. During his time in Newfoundland James Cook carried out a survey of the island's coastline, and John Cartwright made his well-known exploration of the Exploits River system.

animals by fishermen and settlers in Newfoundland and shot on sight. In Palliser's time many of them had already died, and those still living suffered from diseases which they had caught from white men. It would take too long to tell the story here, but perhaps your teacher will tell you of Palliser's efforts to befriend the Beothucks and explain why they failed.

When Palliser returned to England, he tried to persuade the government to make new laws that would completely destroy all settlement and encourage more English ships to go to Newfoundland each year. At last he succeeded, and Palliser's Act was passed by Parliament.

This act forbade fishing ships to carry passengers to Newfoundland. It ordered captains of fishing vessels to bring back to England in the autumn every man they had carried out to

Newfoundland in the spring. Captains who had servants were allowed to hold back half of their wages until the servants returned to England.

To encourage fishing vessels to come to Newfoundland, large sums of money were promised to captains of all English ships that would fish on the Grand Banks. Englishmen would be allowed to dry fish on all the shores of Newfoundland except on the French Shore, and all the coast which was so far unsettled would be kept for the use of British ships. No one would be allowed to live there.

Palliser hoped that this act would stop the growth of settlement in Newfoundland and make the settlers who were already there go away. Fortunately for Newfoundland, the terms of this act were not successfully carried out.

Explore and Discover

1. With the help of your teacher, find out about Palliser's efforts to help the Beothucks and why he did not succeed. Then write down what you have learned.

2. Why was Labrador added to the territory of Newfoundland?

3. Why did Palliser's Act allow captains to keep half of their servants' wages until the servants returned to England?

4. Have a class debate on the topic: *Sir Hugh Palliser was one of the best naval governors that Newfoundland ever had.* Your teacher will tell you how a debate should be held.

20 The Surrogates

Palliser's Act was not carried out because Britain was at war during twenty-five of the forty years after the act was passed. At first there was a war with the United States and her allies— France, Spain, and Holland. Then there was a very long war with France. Just as had happened during the Seven Years' War, the price of fish rose, very high wages were paid in Newfoundland, and the Royal Navy was too busy to enforce either King William's Act or Palliser's Act. Thousands of settlers from England and Ireland flocked to Newfoundland, and when the wars ended in 1815, there were perhaps forty thousand people on the island.

During the wars British shipowners lost interest in sending ships to catch fish in Newfoundland. They had found that they could earn far more money if they bought fish from the settlers and sold it to Spain and Portugal. Therefore the fishery was at last completely controlled by Newfoundlanders.

Still the settlers and the thousands of servants and sharemen who had come from Ireland and England were shamefully treated by merchants and traders. They were not given the protection which proper law courts gave British subjects in other colonies. Since very few fishing ships now came from England, there were not even fishing admirals to enforce justice. The justices of the peace were usually themselves merchants, and they made sure that the laws suited them.

For small offences settlers could be lashed with the cat-o'-nine tails, put in the stocks, or lose all their belongings. For stealing they could have their hands branded or they could be hanged.

Moreover, the British government still told the naval governors not to regard Newfoundland as a colony and to discourage the settlers as much as possible. One British Prime Minister, Lord North, said that whatever they loved to have roasted, he would give it to them raw, and whatever they wished to have raw, he would give it to them roasted.

The governors found it more and more difficult to do their work properly. They knew that many of the merchants who acted as justices of the peace were unfair to the settlers, but they had no one to help them. Soon the governors themselves began to act as judges. Since they could not visit all the outports each summer, they ordered young naval officers serving on ships in Newfoundland waters to sail along the coast and to act as judges wherever they were needed. These naval officers acting as judges were called surrogates.

The surrogates knew how to run warships, but they did not know how to deal with ordinary people who had broken the law. On warships the sailors were not supposed to argue with their officers or disobey orders. The surrogates treated the settlers as they treated sailors on their ships. Although many of their judgements were fair, the punishments they gave were very severe. They used the "cat-o'-nine tails" often.

At last complaints began to reach the British Parliament. The Parliament asked lawyers to investigate, and the lawyers reported that neither the governor nor the surrogates had any right to act as judges. They also said that most courts in Newfoundland were not properly run.

Explore and Discover

1. Who were the surrogates? Find two reasons why they were chosen to act as judges in Newfoundland.
2. Imagine that you were a settler accused of breaking a fishery law at the time when both fishing admirals and surrogates acted as judges. You have the choice of being tried in court by a fishing admiral or by a surrogate. Think of as many reasons as you can for and against each choice and make a list of them.
3. Do you think Newfoundland settlers benefited because fishing ships were no longer sent to Newfoundland? Discuss this question with your teacher and write down what you learn.

21 The Establishment of Courts

When Parliament found out what had been happening in Newfoundland, it demanded that proper courts should be established. The West Country merchants tried to prevent this because, they said, courts would encourage people to stay in Newfoundland. They were afraid that proper courts would take the side of the servants and poor fishermen. Thus merchants would not be able to do exactly as they wished and would not earn as much money as they had earned in the past.

However, Parliament paid no attention to the merchants and, in 1791, a Supreme Court was established in St. John's. The first Chief Justice was John Reeves, an excellent judge and a very hard-working one.

The court was set up for one year only. During that year Chief Justice Reeves studied the situation in Newfoundland. He learned that the settlers were badly treated and that the West Country merchants were selfish. He advised Parliament that permanent courts should be created.

Soon a permanent Supreme Court was established and those accused of crimes could claim trial by jury. Reeves had stated also that there were no suitable persons to appoint as magistrates in the outports. Only merchants, clergymen, and doctors had enough education to act as judges, and none of them would do a good job. The merchants would favour themselves,

The old Court House of St. John's shown in this photograph stood on the same site as the present Court House. Today, as when the court was first established, the chief justice and the judges still go on circuit.

and the clergymen and doctors would be afraid to offend the merchants from whom they got all their money. Throughout the year, the merchants paid the clergymen and doctors on the fishermen's behalf and charged the fees to the fishermen's accounts. The fishermen themselves had no money. They paid the merchants with fish at the end of each fishing season.

Thus Reeves suggested that the surrogates should be allowed to continue to act as magistrates in the outports. They did not know the law very well and were sometimes cruel, but, Reeves said, they would at least be fair and treat everyone the same way. Parliament agreed to this also.

Still, Newfoundlanders were far from satisfied. The new courts operated only during the fishing season, and usually the

80

judges were not able to do their jobs very well. The surrogates were often cruel. Moreover, the chief justice and the surrogates were in Newfoundland only during the summer months. The British government itself was busy because Britain was at war with France. Since Britain did not wish to be bothered with Newfoundland affairs, she sent out the kind of governor who would not complain. These governors often ordered houses to be torn down, garden fences to be destroyed, and settlers to be sent back to England and Ireland. Above all, the British government had still not recognized Newfoundland as a colony.

We can see, therefore, that the establishment of the courts had not made life for the Newfoundland settlers happy and secure. But the courts were important because they had been set up against the wishes of the West Country merchants. For once the merchants had not had their own way, and the settlers believed that this was a good sign for the future.

Explore and Discover

1. Discuss with your teacher what "trial by jury" means. How would trial by jury be more fair for the settlers than trial by fishing admirals and surrogates?

2. Imagine that you were Justice John Reeves and write a report to the British Parliament telling about the treatment of the Newfoundland settlers.

3. Why did Reeves believe that the surrogates should continue to act as judges?

4. Discuss with your teacher why the establishment of courts helped the settlers. Then discuss the ways in which courts in Newfoundland were still not as good as they should have been.

22   After the War

While the war lasted, there was great prosperity in Newfoundland and many new settlers came to share in it. But when the war ended, the price of fish fell. Thousands of fishermen were unemployed and could get no supplies from the merchants, many of whom were themselves bankrupt. For several winters there was so much ice in the harbour of St. John's that the sealing ships were unable to leave port. There were riots in St. John's and also in some outports when hungry people attempted to take food from merchants' stores. To make matters worse, fires burned more than three hundred houses in St. John's. The winter of 1818 was the worst of all and was called "the winter of the rals" or, as we would say, the winter of the rowdies.

The merchants, who were very worried that the "rals" would destroy their property, advised the British government that at least 5,000 settlers should be forced to leave Newfoundland. When this advice was refused, some merchants, helped by the governors, decided to do something themselves. Thousands of unfortunates were shipped back to Ireland. Some were sent to Nova Scotia and Prince Edward Island until these colonies protested that they would not take any more.

The only bright spot in all those years was the appointment of Francis Forbes as Chief Justice. Forbes was the first properly qualified judge to be appointed in nearly thirty years. He boldly declared himself on the side of the settlers and attacked the governors for keeping from Newfoundlanders the rights which all civilized people enjoyed. He ruled that it was silly to reserve all the coastline for fishing ships which did not exist, and he gave settlers the right to build on any part of the shore which was not already occupied. He also ruled that settlers should be allowed to clear land for gardens and farms and for other purposes not connected with the fishery.

The governor was angry with Forbes. He wrote to the British government, hoping that it would not allow the new rules made by the Chief Justice. But the British government was beginning to see that to ignore Newfoundland was foolish. In fact, it now agreed that a governor should live in Newfoundland all year round. Soon the island would be recognized as a colony.

During the cold winter of 1818 many immigrants came to St. John's but could not find work. Many of the inhabitants themselves lacked proper clothing and shelter. In order to obtain food, these men looted shops.

Explore and Discover

1. Imagine that you were a fisherman living in St. John's during "the winter of the rals". Write a story about what happened.

2. Imagine that you were a merchant living in St. John's at the same time and write a letter to the governor telling what you think should be done with the settlers. Give reasons for your plans.

3. Make a list of all the reasons why Newfoundlanders today think very highly of Chief Justice Forbes.

4. Discuss with your teacher why the merchants in Newfoundland wanted to reserve the coast for fishing ships even though West Country fishermen were no longer coming to Newfoundland.

5. With the help of your teacher, make a list of the reasons why you think the British government was beginning to understand that it could no longer pretend Newfoundland was not a colony.

23 Newfoundland Becomes a Colony

The British government was very slowly changing its attitude towards Newfoundland. But the old laws still remained. The governor now lived in Newfoundland all year round. But all the governors were naval officers, and most of them behaved as if they were commanding a ship. They did not allow anyone to question or to criticize them. In fact, they behaved as if they were dictators. Officials were given jobs because they had powerful friends in England or because they were the governor's friends. No one seemed to care whether such officials could do their jobs properly or not.

In the past most Newfoundland settlers had been poor fishermen with little or no education. They could do nothing about the power of the governors and the surrogates. But when the war with France ended in 1815, there were many Newfoundlanders who were well educated and who were determined that their new home should have the same benefits as other British colonies.

Among these men was Dr. William Carson. He was born in Scotland but came to Newfoundland at the age of thirty-eight. He soon saw that Newfoundland was badly governed. He was a brave and unselfish man and fought year after year to have Newfoundland recognized as a proper colony. Through his actions, he made enemies of the governor and all the other officials and lost his job as doctor of the garrison. He wrote pamphlets saying that Newfoundland was badly governed. He said that Newfoundlanders should now be allowed to manage their own affairs and that all British subjects should have the right to elect their own representatives to govern them. After a few years he was able to gather together a group of men who were willing to work with him and fight for better treatment for Newfoundland.

Among these men was a very able young Irishman named Patrick Morris. He had come to Newfoundland at the age of eleven and had become a merchant in St. John's. He was a good speaker with a ready Irish wit, and he loved argument. Like Carson, he published pamphlets. In them he made fun of the way in which Newfoundland was governed. He also attacked the judges and governors who acted in a high-handed

Morris helped Newfoundland to become a colony by writing pamphlets and speaking at meetings. Later he threatened that Newfoundlanders would join the United States if Britain did not grant Responsible Government.

manner. He used all of Carson's arguments, but he wrote and spoke in a much livelier manner.

Many people, including members of the British Parliament, read Morris's and Carson's pamphlets. For the first time many of them realized that Newfoundland's affairs were badly managed. However, it was the cruel acts of the surrogates that finally persuaded Parliament to give Newfoundland a different kind of government.

One day in Harbour Grace two fishermen were summoned to appear before the surrogate. They were late in arriving and were charged with contempt of court. For this they were sentenced to thirty-six lashes on the bare back with a cat-o'-nine tails.

Patrick Morris called a public meeting about the cruel treatment of these fishermen. A petition was sent to the British government. Chief Justice Forbes supported the petition. He said that the surrogates were not only cruel but that they were bad judges. The surrogates seemed to make their own laws and to invent their own punishments.

Parliament now discussed Newfoundland affairs for the first time in thirty years. In 1824 it passed a law which abolished the surrogate system and put in its place the Supreme Court which Newfoundland now has. The new Supreme Court consisted of a chief justice and two assistant judges. Each year the court would go on circuit, that is, travel to various places in Newfoundland where trials would be held. Another law passed in the same year said that King William's Act, Palliser's Act, and all the old fishery laws no longer applied. In the future the governor was to do all he could to encourage settlement, to make grants of land, and to assist settlers in cultivating the land.

The next year a new governor, Sir Thomas Cochrane, was

instructed to set up a council of five men who would assist and advise him. At long last, after more than three hundred years of struggle, Newfoundland had become a colony.

Explore and Discover

1. What is a dictator? How were the governors of Newfoundland like dictators?
2. What kind of men in Newfoundland wanted to change the way Newfoundland was governed?
3. How did William Carson and Patrick Morris tell people in England that Newfoundland was badly governed? By what other means did they try to change the government?
4. Discuss with your teacher the reasons why you think the British Parliament paid a great deal of attention to the cruel treatment of the two fishermen.
5. Why was it necessary for the chief justice and the two judges to go on circuit every year?
6. As a class project, make a pamphlet for the year 1824. Your pamphlet should include articles about all the old laws that the British Parliament changed and the new laws that it made. Explain how each change would benefit Newfoundland settlers.

24 Village Settlements

In spite of many difficulties thousands of settlers had made Newfoundland their home. Villages were now scattered along the whole coast, in coves and on offshore islands that were near fishing grounds. It was important to be near good fishing grounds because engines had not yet been invented, and the fishermen went to sea in boats that had only oars and sails.

Most of the coastal villages were small. In some of them there was only a single family; few villages had more than a hundred inhabitants. Some villages were occupied only during the summer months. When autumn came, fishermen often left the bleak islands and headlands and moved to the deep bays where the forest provided shelter and firewood. Here they lived until spring in log houses which they called "tilts".

Many of these small villages had no shops, schools, churches, or post offices. There were no roads, and the railway had not yet been built. The only way to travel was by boat. Thus many people lived all their lives without leaving their own village.

But life in the villages was very busy. During the fishing season the day's work would begin before dawn. The men and older boys spent the days on the fishing grounds. When they returned, the fish that had been caught had to be cleaned, split, and salted. The women helped with this work, which was often finished by the light of cod-oil torches. When fish was very plentiful, the women worked all day in the stages.

To make soap the settlers first obtained a supply of hardwood ash, which was stored in a dry place. Then water was run slowly through the ash to dissolve the potash. This water containing potash was called lye. It was boiled together with tallow from meat fat in a large iron kettle to make "soft" soap. To make "hard" soap, some salt was added to the mixture.

Later in the season the fish had to be washed and spread on the flakes for drying. Both the women and the children worked hard at this task. Each morning the fish was spread out, and each evening, or at any time when rain threatened to fall, it had to be gathered into piles on the flakes. There was hardly a moment of the day when there was not something to be done, until at last the fish had been dried and taken to the merchant to be exchanged for the winter's provisions.

Of course, there was a great deal to be done apart from the catching and curing of fish. Most families had gardens where they grew potatoes, cabbages, carrots, turnips, and other vegetables. Many people kept a few sheep, some chickens, and perhaps a pig or two. The animals had to be cared for, and hay had to be cut, dried, and stored as winter feed for the sheep. Most of this work was done by the women. But the women also had to keep their families clothed and look after various household tasks. They cooked over wood fires and in open fireplaces. They made their own soap from fat and wood ashes. They also carded and spun the wool of their sheep to knit into warm clothing.

During the winter months the men cut fire-wood, as well as timber for the building of houses, stages, wharves, stores, flakes, and boats. Winter was also the season to hunt the sea birds, seals, and caribou that, in many cases, provided the only fresh meat to be had. New fishing equipment was made, and old equipment was repaired in order that all might be ready for the fishing season when springtime came again.

Despite all this hard work, most fishermen earned a poor living, and many of them lived all their lives without seeing money. In the spring, those who owned their boats and fishing equipment would get from a merchant the summer's fishery supplies and food for the summer. In return they promised to bring the merchant in the autumn all the fish they would catch during the summer. With this fish they paid both for the supplies which they had taken in the spring and also for food for the winter. Often there was not enough fish to pay for all the food and supplies. The fishermen were then in debt to the merchant. Many fishermen spent all their lives in debt.

The merchants too were often in debt. Because they knew that some fishermen would never be able to pay all their bills, they charged very high prices for the goods they sold. But when they were not able to collect enough fish to pay for all the supplies they had received, they became bankrupt.

Explore and Discover

1. Imagine that you were a member of a fisherman's family living in a small Newfoundland outport one hundred and fifty years ago. Choose one season of the year and make a list of the most important jobs that you and other members of your family would have to do.

2. Discuss with your teacher what is meant by the "credit system". Discuss also how this system might have helped the fishermen and how it might have harmed them. Then write down what you learn.

3. Why do you think the merchants charged high prices for their goods even though they knew the fishermen would not be able to repay them with fish?

25 St. John's and the Outports

The merchants in the smaller villages usually got their supplies
from more important merchants in the larger outports or in St.
John's. St. John's was then a town with a population of about
twelve thousand. The main street, now called Water Street,
was then known as the Lower Path. It was narrow, crooked,
and very muddy.

Along the waterfront were the stores and wharves of the
merchants. Here ships and boats of all sizes landed fish, seal-
skins, and oil collected from the outports. In exchange, they
took food, provisions, and fishing supplies which they carried
round the coast. Here, too, ships loaded dried fish to take to
ports in Spain, Portugal, Italy, South America, and the West
Indies. On their return voyages they brought salt, cork, oil, and
wines from the Mediterranean, molasses and rum from the
West Indies, and salt beef, pork, flour, and other foodstuffs, as
well as clothing and fishing supplies from England, Ireland,
and the United States.

In St. John's might also be seen ships of the Royal Navy. The
governor, the judges of the Supreme Court, the Collector of
Customs, and other officials lived there, as well as a garrison
of soldiers. The officers of the garrison, the government officials,
and the principal merchants lived very comfortably in fine
houses. They owned beautiful furniture and good libraries and
enjoyed good food and wine. But most of them did not regard

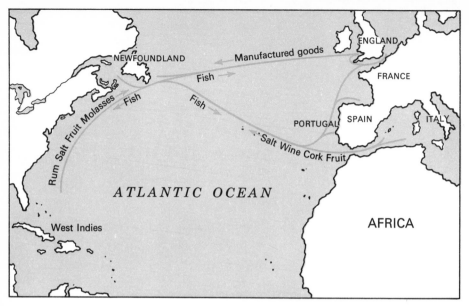

For a long time the fish trade was Newfoundland's only source of money. The firmest and whitest fish was sent to the Mediterranean and Europe, and the poorer fish was shipped to the slave-owners in the West Indies. In return Newfoundlanders received manufactured goods, foodstuffs, and rum. The fish trade enabled them to buy delicacies such as fresh fruit and wine.

Newfoundland as their home. When they retired, they went back to England. For this reason they were not greatly interested in making St. John's a beautiful town.

The majority of the people of St. John's lived in wooden houses on the side of the steep hill that rose from the harbour. Only narrow, muddy lanes separated the rows of houses and whenever a fire broke out, there was danger that many homes would be destroyed.

Not many people in St. John's were fishermen. Most of the men worked for the merchants as servants or as labourers. A few had begun to clear land and make small farms, raising vegetables and animals which they sold in the town. Others worked in coopers' shops, making barrels and casks in which fish was packed for export. Some men made sails for the many ships which came to St. John's. Others owned taverns and sold rum to the sailors who visited the port, as well as to the inhabitants.

But there were also many unemployed people in St. John's, particularly in the winter months when the waterfront was not busy. Also, many men who worked in the fishery during the summer came to St. John's in the winter, hoping to find enough work to pay for their food and shelter until spring. Many were not able to find work.

Among the outports, the largest were Harbour Grace, Carbonear, Trinity, Bonavista, Fogo, Twillingate, Harbour Breton, and Belleoram. Each of these ports was the headquarters of at least one important merchant. However, most of the people in the outports were fishermen. Some of them

The drawing below shows a cooper tightening the rope round the upper part of the barrel so that a hoop may be finally put round the staves.

This drawing shows St. John's around 1840. The sacks the men are carrying and the barrels in the foreground were the chief containers in which goods were packed.

owned their own boats and equipment and were known as planters. Others were servants who hired themselves to planters or merchants for wages or a share of the fish. Many of the planters were prosperous and happy. The servants were usually very poor. In Harbour Grace and Carbonear there were, as in St. John's, many unemployed people.

At this time in Newfoundland, then, there were a few wealthy and powerful merchants and a great many more small merchants and prosperous planters. The majority of the people, however, were very poor and had to work hard to earn a living.

Explore and Discover

1. Think of all the ways Newfoundlanders depended on fish and make a list of them. Then, with the help of your teacher, try to find out all the purposes for which fish is used today.
2. Imagine that you were an English visitor in St. John's about one hundred and fifty years ago. Write a letter home to England telling what you have seen and whom you have met.

26   The Spread of Settlement

Settlement had spread along the coast of Newfoundland until there were as many as thirteen hundred separate settlements. We might ask why so many settlers wanted to make Newfoundland their home. It would be true to say that they came to catch fish, because for many years the fishery was the only industry in Newfoundland, but this would not be the whole truth.

Some men came to Newfoundland because they thought that they could earn a great deal of money by exchanging provisions for fish and then selling the fish to people overseas. That is to say, they came to trade.

Other people came because they were unhappy at home in England or Ireland. Some could not earn a living there and thought that they could work as servants in Newfoundland and perhaps save enough money to buy their own boats and equipment. Others had been badly treated and thought that they would be happier in a new land, living in a small village where no one could trouble them. Still others had not been allowed to practise their religion and thought that they would find religious freedom in the new land.

Among the settlers were also men who had not wanted to serve in the Royal Navy, as well as men who had run away from harsh masters or cruel naval officers. Some were criminals who hoped to hide from the law in Newfoundland.

For all these reasons, and perhaps for others that you can think of, settlers came to Newfoundland. There were also many reasons why the settlers chose to live in hundreds of small settlements rather than in one or two large towns.

First of all, they wanted to live near the sea. They needed a good harbour that would provide shelter for their boats and buildings. They wanted enough space on the waterfront to build their wharves, stages, stores, and flakes. They also needed fresh water and wood for building and for fuel. Finally, they wanted to be as near as possible to good fishing grounds.

Most of the harbours in Newfoundland were large enough for only ten or twelve stages and wharves, and many of the fishing grounds, too, were small. Therefore, as the number of settlers grew, they had to spread out.

Many settlers came in fishing or trading ships from England and Ireland. Some of these ships sailed directly to St. John's or to other ports on the Avalon Peninsula. Other ships went to ports in Trinity, Bonavista, or Notre Dame Bays or to the South Coast harbours. In this way the settlers were scattered far and wide from the start.

Many settlers, of course, wanted to be far away from the main settlements. The deserters from the Royal Navy and the law-breakers wanted to hide from the law. Some people wanted to live by themselves. Others wanted to own a large amount of land or to have a whole harbour to themselves. Some people moved away from the main settlements because they hoped that there would be more fish in the next bay and that life there would be easier.

The merchants also had their reasons for establishing their businesses in different outport communities. Each merchant wanted to be able to collect fish from a large number of fisher-

In this photograph the S.S. *Kyle*, a coastal steamer, is shown entering Trinity harbour. Boats have always been an important means of transportation for Newfoundlanders, because even as late as 1850 there were few proper roads outside the area around St. John's.

The photograph below shows a view of modern Trinity. One of Newfoundland's oldest settlements, Trinity dates from the time that Lord Falkland tried to found a plantation near the present town. At one time an important commercial centre, it is today a quiet fishing village.

men and to sell supplies to them. Each wanted as little competition as possible from the other merchants.

There is at least one other reason why the settlers built their homes where they did. They came to Newfoundland from the West Country counties of England—Devon, Dorset, Cornwall, and Somerset—as well as from Ireland. The newcomers wanted to settle among people they knew or, at least, among people who spoke the same dialect, had the same customs, and practised the same religion. Most of the Irish settlers, for example, chose to live on the Avalon Peninsula. Although many settlers moved from the place where they first came to live, the isolation of most Newfoundland villages often kept speech and customs unchanged for many years.

People living in different districts today still have their own dialects and their own customs. They sing different folk songs and have different dances. They even build different boats and use different fishing methods.

Explore and Discover

1. Discuss the reasons why people settled in your town or village.

2. As a class project, make a book of Newfoundland songs. Find one song for each country that Newfoundlanders came from—England, Ireland, Scotland, Wales, and France, for example. Then find one song for each of the main occupations—fishing, seal hunting, logging, and so on. Include any songs that were written or are sung often in your own town or village.

3. Make a map of your town or village and the area around it. Mark the names of all the coves, harbours, rocks, capes, islands, ponds, rivers, and brooks. Try to find out where the names came from.

27 The Seal Hunt

Most Newfoundland settlers were inshore fishermen. That is, they fished near the shore in small boats, landing their catch each day and returning to their homes each night. Some men fished alone, but other boats carried as many as six or seven men.

There were also fishermen who went to the Grand Banks in large schooners which stayed at sea for two or three weeks at a time. Others fished on nearer banks in small schooners called western boats, jack boats, or bully boats. Still others went to live each summer on the coast of Labrador and returned with their catch in the autumn.

Many young Newfoundland sailors served on ships which carried fish to the Mediterranean and West Indian markets. Others served on whaling ships, many of which were owned by people in Scotland.

Every year, however, the month of March saw the beginning of an adventure for fishermen of the East Coast particularly. This was the annual seal hunt.

Each autumn when the Arctic winter approaches, large herds of harp and hood seals move southward, passing the coast of Newfoundland and Labrador. When spring comes, they turn northward again. Off the coast of Newfoundland and southern Labrador, they meet the great ice floes which are carried southward by the Labrador Current. The seals clamber onto the floes, and here the young seals, or "white-coats", are born.

The pelts of the whitecoats were very valuable, because large amounts of useful oil could be made from the fat. Also, the skin could be made into a very fine leather. The rich seal meat, moreover, was very welcome in Newfoundland outports where other kinds of fresh meat were hard to get.

Thus from very early times Newfoundlanders tried to catch the seals passing the coast. In the autumn and early winter the seals were caught in nets. But when the seals on the floating ice fields were brought near the land, men from the shore either walked or rowed in small boats to the seal herds. There the hunters killed the seals, removed the pelts, and towed the seals and the pelts back to the shore.

However the ice fields did not always bring the seal herds near the land. For this reason, the hunters began to build larger boats which could sail far enough to find the herds. At one time up to four hundred ships carrying thirteen thousand seal hunters would go each year "to the ice". Later large steel ships with powerful engines were built.

Seal hunting was a great adventure, but it was also a very dangerous occupation. Sometimes the moving ice fields crushed even the stoutest ships. Men could be separated from their ships by moving ice or lose their way in blizzards. In the *Greenland* disaster fifty-two men were separated from their ship in a bad storm and perished on the ice, as did seventy-seven men of the crew of the *Newfoundland*. The loss of the *Southern Cross* with all her crew is still sadly remembered in story and song, as is the destruction of the *Viking*. Hundreds of ships and many lives were lost "at the ice", but there were always young men eager to join the sealing fleet and share in the great adventure.

The seal hunt was very important because the sealers could earn extra money. The hunt took place in the spring, before the cod fishery had begun. At this time the fishermen's winter supplies were getting low, and the money earned from the seal hunt enabled fishermen to feed and clothe their families. In a good year there was enough money left over to buy equipment for the summer fishery.

The sealing ships, which were very strongly built for sailing through ice fields, were always in demand for use in the Arctic and Antarctic Oceans. Famous explorers such as Sir Robert Scott and Admiral Byrd used Newfoundland sealing ships on their expeditions.

The first settlers hunted seals in the autumn with nets made from strong twine. The nets were about forty fathoms long and three fathoms deep. The spring seal hunt did not become a large operation until around 1840.

Today the seal hunt is a very small operation, since seal oil is no longer in great demand and man-made materials have replaced seal-skin leather. But the great seal hunt remains an adventurous chapter in Newfoundland's past.

Explore and Discover

1. Collect pictures of different kinds of seals that live in the Canadian Arctic and find out as much as you can about how they live. If you write to the Department of Fisheries, they may be able to help you with this project.
2. Collect as many stories and songs about the seal hunt as you can. Put them together to make a book.

28 Churches and Schools

Although the population of Newfoundland and the number of settlements grew, for many years there were no schools or churches. The British government did not help to build any because it did not treat Newfoundland as a colony and did not wish to encourage settlement. The settlers themselves usually could not read or write and were thus unable to help themselves. The richer merchants sent their children to school in England or elsewhere. Others were able to hire private tutors. But most Newfoundlanders grew up without any schooling and without the services of church or clergy.

Among the people in Britain who thought that churches and schools should be built in Newfoundland were the members of the Society for the Propagation of the Gospel, or the SPG, as it was called. This society was more interested in establishing the Church of England than in education. But they knew that if the people were to take part in church services, they had to be able to read. Therefore, the SPG started schools as well as churches. Altogether, more than twenty schools were established. Many of them were Sunday schools, for on weekdays the older boys and girls had to help with the fishing or the gardening. But in the Sunday schools, as well as in the day schools, the pupils learned reading, writing, and arithmetic as well as religious knowledge.

This photograph shows the Arts and Administration building of the Memorial University of Newfoundland, which was established in 1949 and is Newfoundland's centre for higher education. The university offers degrees in arts, science, education, and commerce. In 1968 it had over 6,000 students. The Government of Newfoundland gives financial aid to students and also helps some students to study at other universities outside the province.

The first SPG school was started in Bonavista in 1726. Forty years later the first Methodist missionary to Newfoundland started a school at Harbour Grace. Soon several other Methodist schools were built.

Twenty years after the coming of the Methodists, the Roman Catholic people were allowed to have their own priests with them in Newfoundland. Soon Catholics were thinking of building schools. About twenty years later two new societies were formed. They were the St. John's Charity School Society and the Benevolent Irish Society. Both these societies established schools in St. John's for poor children of all religions. But within a short time the schools of the Benevolent Irish Society became schools which only Roman Catholic children attended. Soon the boys were put under the care of the Christian Brothers of Ireland, and when Bishop Fleming came to Newfoundland, he arranged for Sisters of the Presentation Order and of the Order of Mercy to take charge of the education of Roman Catholic girls.

About the same time an English merchant founded the Newfoundland School Society. This society collected money in Newfoundland and received some from England as well. It established many schools throughout the island. Although at first the society was intended for people of all religions, it soon became a Church of England organization.

When Newfoundland finally got its own government, an event which we shall read about in the next chapters, that government decided to help educate Newfoundland children. School boards were set up throughout Newfoundland, and money was given for the building of schools and the hiring of teachers. The government hoped that children of all religions would go to the same schools. But the schools had been built and operated for many years by the different churches, and it was difficult to change the old habits. For this reason, among others, the government decided after a few years to give money to the different churches and to allow them to run the schools. In this way our present school system began.

Because Newfoundlanders have always lived in many small, isolated communities, it has been very difficult for the churches and the government to provide good schools and good teachers. Moreover, until very recently, no law required Newfoundland children to attend school. Parents who were themselves uneducated thought that their sons would grow up to be fishermen and their daughters would be fishermen's wives. They did not always think that education was necessary. Therefore many children did not go to school at all. Others often stayed at home to help with the fish, to plant or dig potatoes, or to pick berries.

The children who went to school often left at a very early age to join a fishing crew or to go to sea. Others learned very little because the teachers themselves were poorly educated.

While hard-working missionaries of all religions were bringing education to Newfoundland, others were bringing spiritual help to the lonely villages. Priests and clergy underwent great hardships. At a time when there were no roads, railways, or steamships, they travelled in all seasons along the coasts of Newfoundland. There were never enough missionaries for the task. Often the travelling was so difficult and the territory missionaries had to cover was so great that they could not manage to visit all their parishioners even once a year.

Explore and Discover

1. Talk to the oldest people you know and ask them to tell you about the schools they went to when they were children. Then discuss with your teacher what you have learned.
2. Why was it difficult to set up good schools in Newfoundland?
3. Try to find out the history of your school and write down what you learn.
4. Explain how churches came to be responsible for education in Newfoundland. Why were the first schools started by church organizations?

29 Missionaries in Labrador

In the time of Governor Palliser, a society known as the Moravian Mission asked permission to come to work among the Eskimos in Labrador. Governor Palliser was pleased to support the Moravian Mission's request. He hoped that it would keep the Eskimos away from the Labrador coast so that English fishermen could work without fear of being attacked.

The Moravians believed that the Eskimos should be protected from traders who wanted to sell them rum, brandy, and guns at very high prices. Most of the traders came to harbours in southern Labrador and northern Newfoundland. Every year many Eskimos travelled south to visit the traders and neglected their fishing and hunting. When winter came, they often went hungry and many of them died of starvation. The Moravians hoped to keep the Eskimos in the north. For this reason they built their mission stations at Nain, Hopedale, Hebron, Makkovik, Okak, and Ramah. They also built trading posts so that the Eskimos would not need to travel south.

The task of the Moravians was a difficult one. The Eskimos worshipped their own gods and were not eager to change their way of life. But after many years they were converted to Christianity and no longer went south to meet the traders. Because the missionaries were happy with their work, they were able to bear the loneliness of living in northern Labrador, the cold winter climate, and the separation from their children who were sent to school in Europe.

The Moravians preached the gospel to the Eskimos and traded with them. They also built schools and provided simple medical care. Slowly the Eskimos changed their ways. They ceased to be wandering hunters and settled near the mission stations.

The Moravians still continue their good work in Labrador today. In Canada's Centennial Year, Eskimo children from the Moravian school at Nain won a prize for a mural which they made.

The Indians of Labrador, like the Eskimos, were a wandering people. In some ways they were like the Beothucks, but instead of hunting along the sea-shore in summer they visited the coast only to trade. There they exchanged furs for supplies. They depended on the caribou for their food, clothing, and shelter. On their hunting and trading expeditions they travelled across Labrador, from the coast to Quebec, and so met French-speaking Roman Catholic missionaries who converted them to Christianity. Each year they travelled to Seven Islands or some other Quebec town to attend the church services. The Indians, too, have now given up many of their old ways. Most of them live in comfortable, new houses at North West River or Davis Inlet. These houses have been built by the Newfoundland government and the federal government of Canada.

But Eskimos and Indians were not the only inhabitants of Labrador. Slowly the southern coast was settled in much the same way as had been the coast of Newfoundland. Some settlers came directly from England, while others came from Newfoundland. Each summer large numbers of Newfoundland fishermen came to the Labrador coast, and some of them decided to stay.

Nain, the first Moravian Mission station on the Labrador coast, was established in 1771 by a few missionaries. By 1900 the population of all the mission stations included about 1,500 Eskimos and 26 missionaries.

Those who settled on the Labrador coast lived a lonely and difficult life. There were no doctors, teachers, or clergy. The long winters were often times of hunger. Many of the summer fishermen also suffered because no medical help was available.

In 1892 an organization in England, the Board of Deep Sea Missions, decided to send a hospital ship to Labrador. On that ship sailed Dr. Wilfred Grenfell, who was to devote the rest of

111

his life to the people of Labrador and northern Newfoundland.

Dr. Grenfell soon saw that one hospital ship was not enough. Labrador needed many hospitals and nursing stations but had no money to build and operate them. Dr. Grenfell set out to raise money in the United States and Canada. He wrote books and travelled to give lectures. Everywhere he told the story of Labrador and asked for help.

Dr. Grenfell's tours were very successful, and the work of the Grenfell Mission grew rapidly. A large, modern hospital was built at the Mission's headquarters in St. Anthony. Other hospitals and nursing stations were built on the Labrador coast. Well-trained doctors and nurses from England, Canada, and the United States came to serve in these hospitals and stations and to man the new hospital ship, a gift from Lord Strathcona. Boarding schools were built, and some of the students who graduated from them were given scholarships by schools and colleges in the United States and Canada. An orphanage was built in St. Anthony.

Thus Dr. Grenfell brought medical care and education to the Labrador coast and to northern Newfoundland. He also helped to chart the Labrador coast and persuaded the New-foundland government to build lighthouses at dangerous points along the coast. He helped to raise money for the building of a dock at St. Anthony and started a handicrafts industry that helped many poor people to earn a better living.

Dr. Grenfell was the last great missionary in Newfoundland. We owe a debt of gratitude to him and to men such as Father Sears and J. J. Curling, who took the whole West Coast for their parishes, and William Marshall, the untiring Methodist missionary. The work of all the societies and, in later years, the work of the Salvation Army have done much to make Newfoundland a better place in which to live. Newfound-

The four-storey hospital in St. Anthony shown here is one of several hospitals established by Dr. Grenfell. Dr. Grenfell also founded nursing stations and obtained hospital ships that travelled around the coast of northern Newfoundland and Labrador, bringing medical aid to isolated settlements.

The photograph below shows the *Northern Ranger,* a coastal mail and passenger ship, docked at St. Anthony, the Grenfell Labrador Mission station that serves northern Newfoundland and the coast of Labrador. The children shown in the foreground are from the Mission's orphanage in St. Anthony.

landers perhaps owe more to the missionaries, many of whose names we do not even know, than to all the famous explorers and governors of the past.

Explore and Discover

1. Why did the Moravian missionaries try to keep the Eskimos away from the coast of Labrador?

2. Find out as much as you can about the work of the Moravian missionaries in Newfoundland and Labrador today. Discuss their work with your teacher and your classmates.

3. Make a list of all the ways in which Dr. Grenfell helped the people of Newfoundland and Labrador. Why do you think he came to work with them?

4. How did Dr. Grenfell obtain money to carry on the work of the Grenfell Mission?

5. With the help of your teacher, try to find out about the lives of any of the missionaries, other than Dr. Grenfell, who worked in Newfoundland and Labrador.

30 Representative Government

Newfoundlanders were pleased that Newfoundland was at last a colony, but they were not satisfied. They wanted to elect their own government.

For seven years, led by Dr. William Carson and Patrick Morris, they continued the struggle. Finally in 1832 Governor Cochrane was ordered by the British government to arrange for the election of an assembly.

The island was divided into nine districts from which altogether fifteen men were to be elected. Every man who was over twenty-one years of age and had lived in Newfoundland for one year could vote.

Today voting is secret. People cannot find out for whom you vote if you do not tell them. But in 1832 the voter had to walk up to the polling station and announce the name of the man for whom he was voting. Many fights took place at polling stations, and many people were afraid to vote. Some were forced to vote for a candidate whom they did not want. Sometimes candidates hired rowdies to prevent people from voting against them.

When the Assembly had been elected, it was called to meet in St. John's. Governor Cochrane explained the form of the new government. It would have three parts: the Governor, the Council, and the Assembly. The Governor and the Council would be appointed by the British government. The Assembly

The Colonial Building was the home of the Government of Newfoundland from 1847 to 1960. After the Second World War the National Convention met there to debate whether Newfoundland should join Canada.

would be elected. The Assembly would suggest new laws for Newfoundland, and these suggestions would go to the Council. If the Council approved the suggestions, they would go to the Governor. If he signed them, they would become law.

Governor Cochrane told the Assembly that there were many things to be done. Roads and schools had to be built, and lighthouses and fog alarms had to be set up along the coast. Policemen and fire fighters were needed, as well as a savings bank. Many other matters had to be settled so that Newfoundland could become a prosperous, well-run colony.

Cochrane also warned the Assembly that it should not quarrel with the Council. He knew that the elected Assembly represented the poor people and the fishermen, whereas the Council represented wealthy businessmen. He thought that they might not agree, and he was proved right. The Assembly wanted to control all the money, and the Council would not allow it to do so. Soon their quarrel was so serious that no work could be done.

Almost everyone in Newfoundland took sides in this fight between the Assembly and the Council. The Roman Catholic Bishop, Bishop Fleming, was on the side of the Assembly and did everything he could to help it, as did Dr. William Carson. The editor of a St. John's newspaper who supported the Council was so unpopular that he was pulled from his horse while riding between Harbour Grace and Carbonear and had his ears cut off. At every election there were riots.

It seemed that Representative Government, which Newfoundlanders had waited so long to get, would not work. As long as the Council and the Governor had most of the power, the Assembly could do very little.

Explore and Discover

1. Try to find out all the reasons why Newfoundlanders wanted Representative Government and make a list of them.
2. What kind of things do you think the Council and the Assembly wanted to do with the Newfoundlanders' money?
3. Discuss what is meant by a "democratic government". Then write an explanation of why the Representative Government that Newfoundland had been granted was not really democratic.

117

31 Responsible Government

Dr. Carson, Patrick Morris, and their friends, whom we shall call the Reformers, believed that in every free country the people should have the power to govern themselves. They knew, of course, that the people could not all meet to make laws and enforce them. But the people could elect representatives to act for them. If the representatives did not act properly, the people could refuse to vote for them in the next election.

When Representative Government had been granted to Newfoundland, the Reformers had thought the people would at last have their own government. However, they were proved wrong. The Assembly, which represented the people, was prevented from doing what it wished by the Council and the Governor, who were appointed by the British government.

The Reformers soon saw that if the people of Newfoundland were to govern themselves, they had to find a way to make the Governor and the Council do as the Assembly wished. That is, the government they wanted for Newfoundland was the kind we call Responsible Government.

Under Responsible Government the Governor has no real power. He has to do what the Council advises him to do. The Council is chosen from the Assembly, which is elected by the people. Therefore the people have the real power, since they alone can elect the men from whom the Council is chosen and refuse to elect those whom they do not want in the Council or in the Assembly.

The Reformers now told the British government that they would not be satisfied until Newfoundland was given Responsible Government. The Governor opposed this idea because he did not want to lose his power, and the members of the Council knew that they would not be elected and would lose their fine jobs. They tried to persuade the British government to ignore the Reformers.

This chart shows how Responsible Government in Newfoundland worked. The members of the Legislative Council were appointed by the Governor, and the members of the Assembly were elected. Together they made laws for Newfoundland, which the Executive Council enforced.

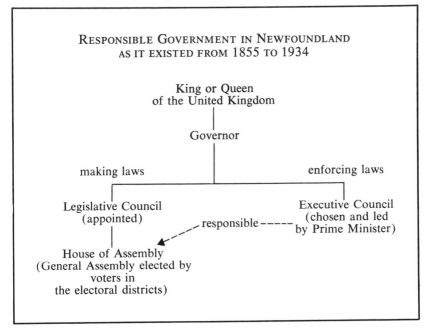

RESPONSIBLE GOVERNMENT IN NEWFOUNDLAND
AS IT EXISTED FROM 1855 TO 1934

King or Queen
of the United Kingdom

Governor

making laws   enforcing laws

Legislative Council   Executive Council
(appointed)   -- responsible ----- (chosen and led
                                               by Prime Minister)
House of Assembly
(General Assembly elected by
voters in
the electoral districts)

119

The Reformers now had a very able leader. He was Philip Francis Little, an Irishman who had come to Newfoundland from Prince Edward Island. Many fishermen and poor people supported him because they believed that they would be treated fairly if the members of the Council were chosen from the Assembly. In England also there were many men in Parliament who believed that the people should rule themselves.

After several years of argument, the British government agreed to do as the Reformers wished. The Governor was told that a new Council would be chosen from the new Assembly soon to be elected. Little, who had been in England, hurried back to Newfoundland to be a candidate in the election.

Newfoundland had now been divided into fifteen districts, which elected a total of thirty members to the Assembly. Little and his followers, whom we may call the Liberal Party, won seventeen seats. Since this was a majority, the Governor had to ask Little to choose the members of the new Council. Little himself became Newfoundland's first Prime Minister. Thus in 1855 Newfoundland finally gained Responsible Government.

Explore and Discover

1. Find out how elections are held and how a government is formed today. Then divide your class into groups to represent different political parties and hold an election. Each party should choose a leader. Your teacher might play the part of the Governor-General and ask the leader of the winning party to form a government.

2. What were the differences between the Representative Government that the Newfoundlanders had had and the Responsible Government that they now had? Think of as many differences as you can and make a list of them.

32　The French Shore

You will remember that when the Treaty of Utrecht was signed, the French were given the right to land and dry their fish on the Newfoundland coast between Cape Bonavista and Point Riche. No French fishermen were allowed to stay in Newfoundland during the winter. After the Seven Years' War the islands of St. Pierre and Miquelon were given to France.

The French had always said that they alone were allowed to fish from their part of the coast. But English fishermen, and Newfoundland fishermen too, said that they could fish wherever they wished, including from the French Shore.

The British government did not wish to annoy France because it feared war might result. It often ordered the governors of Newfoundland and the Royal Navy to help the French keep English and Newfoundland fishermen away from the French Shore.

During the years when Britain and France were at war, French fishermen did not come to Newfoundland because they feared the Royal Navy, which was very strong. Thus Newfoundlanders moved into many unoccupied bays, harbours, coves, and islands. Bonavista Bay and Notre Dame Bay were settled during the Seven Years' War, when the United States and France fought against Britain.

When French fishermen returned to Newfoundland after the

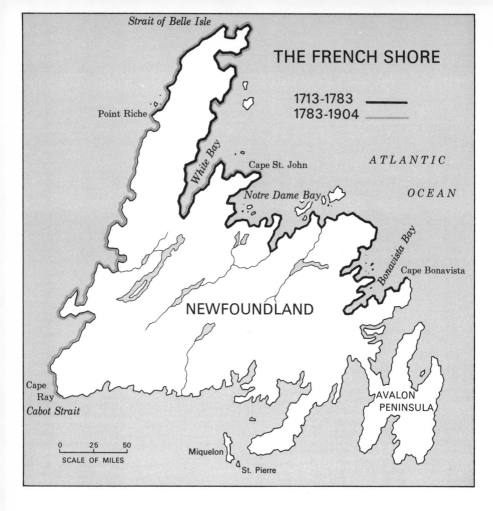

The French Shore

Strait of Belle Isle

THE FRENCH SHORE

1713-1783 ——————
1783-1904 ——————

Point Riche

White Bay

Cape St. John

ATLANTIC

Notre Dame Bay

OCEAN

Bonavista Bay

Cape Bonavista

NEWFOUNDLAND

Cape Ray

Cabot Strait

AVALON PENINSULA

0   25   50
SCALE OF MILES

Miquelon

St. Pierre

wars, they found so many settlers in these bays that they could no longer fish in all the places that they had used in the past. Therefore they agreed that the boundaries of the French Shore should be changed from Cape Bonavista northward to Cape St. John and from Point Riche southward to Cape Ray.

When Newfoundlanders began to govern themselves, they wanted to govern all of Newfoundland, including the French Shore. After a long argument the British government promised that it would never again make an agreement with France

122

about the Newfoundland coast unless the Newfoundland government approved of it.

This promise, however, was not always kept. An agreement was made that allowed the French to catch lobsters and to build lobster factories on the West Coast. The Newfoundland government protested. It claimed that the treaties with France allowed the French fishermen to catch only fish, not lobsters. It said also that the French could use the Newfoundland coast only to dry their fish, but had no right to build factories there.

Newfoundlanders thought it was unfair that the French caught a great deal of fish in Newfoundland which they sold to countries that might otherwise have bought fish from New-

Today Bonavista is an important fishing centre 220 miles from St. John's. It has a fish-drying and cold-storage plant. Both salmon and cod are caught. The picture shows Bonavista about 1960.

In the modern photograph above fishermen are clearing their cod-trap with dip nets. A single catch of cod has been known to weigh over 50,000 pounds.

foundland. Moreover, the best farmland in the island and some of the best woodland were on the French Shore. Newfoundlanders thought that valuable minerals might be found there also. But unless the British government helped them, there was little that Newfoundlanders could do. The British, on their part, were anxious to remain on friendly terms with France.

At last the Newfoundland government decided to take matters into its own hands. It was clear that French fishermen could not catch fish without bait. The French bought or caught most of the herring, caplin, and squid that they needed for bait on the South Coast. The government therefore passed a law which said that no Newfoundlanders should sell bait to French fishermen and that these fishermen should not be allowed to catch bait anywhere except on the French Shore.

For a year or two after this law was passed, the French found it more difficult to catch fish. Then they began to catch more bait on the West Coast. They also brought bait with them from Europe and bought some from Nova Scotia fisher-men. Moreover, many Newfoundlanders were more interested in making money than in obeying the law, and the Newfound-land government did not have enough policemen to enforce the law strictly. Soon the French were catching as much fish as ever.

For many years Newfoundlanders could do nothing about the French Shore. At last Britain saw an opportunity to help. Germany was becoming very powerful, and France feared that one day there might be a war with Germany. In that case, the French would need Britain's help. The British government said that it would agree to help France fight Germany if the French would give up their claim to the French Shore in Newfound-land. France agreed to do so, and in 1904 the agreement was signed.

At last the Newfoundland people had control of the whole island. Only St. Pierre and Miquelon remained French terri-tory, as they do to this day.

Explore and Discover

1. Why did Newfoundlanders not want the French to fish in New-foundland? Find four other reasons why they thought the French Shore should belong to Newfoundland.

2. How did the Government of Newfoundland try to make it difficult for the French to catch fish?

33 Newfoundland Refuses to Join Canada

A little more than one hundred years ago Canada, as we know it today, did not exist. In the territory which we now call Canada, there were seven British colonies: Newfoundland, Nova Scotia, New Brunswick, Prince Edward Island, Canada (now the Provinces of Ontario and Quebec), the Red River Settlement (now the Province of Manitoba), and British Columbia. Most of these provinces were small and poor. They could not afford to build roads and railways, and they were afraid of their powerful neighbour, the United States.

There were many people in each of these colonies who believed that they should unite to form one powerful nation. Then they would be able to build railroads and would be better able to defend themselves in time of war.

In 1864 representatives of Nova Scotia, Prince Edward Island, New Brunswick, and Canada met at Charlottetown to discuss the idea of union, or confederation. Newfoundland was invited to this meeting, but the Prime Minister, Hugh Hoyles, decided not to attend. The delegates to the conference were in favour of confederation and planned to meet again in Quebec City later in the year to work out the details.

The men who attended the meeting in Quebec are called "The Fathers of Confederation". Among them were two New-

The Fathers of Confederation met in Quebec City in 1864 to talk about union of the provinces. Ambrose Shea and Frederick Carter attended the conference, but Newfoundland chose to remain independent at that time.

foundlanders; for though the Prime Minister himself did not attend, he sent Ambrose Shea and Frederick Carter to represent the Newfoundland people. Both Shea and Carter believed that Newfoundland should take part in confederation and join a new Canadian nation.

Many Newfoundlanders, however, did not want to join Canada. They had worked long and hard for the right to govern themselves. They feared that within confederation they might lose that right. Besides, they said, Newfoundlanders had always had close ties with Britain and Europe, but never with Canada.

People who used such arguments were called anti-Confederates. They soon found a leader, a wealthy businessman named Charles Fox Bennett. The Newfoundland government had given Bennett large areas of land in which he hoped to find minerals. Indeed, he had already opened copper mines at Tilt Cove. He feared that if confederation came about, the

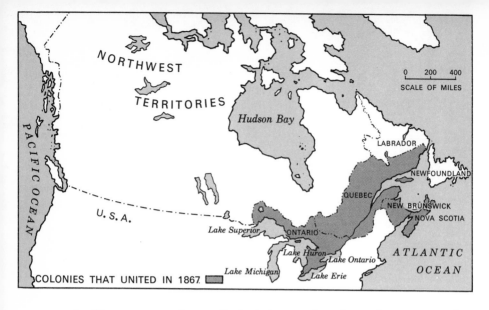

In this map note the small shaded area that shows the provinces that united to form the Dominion of Canada in 1867: Canada, New Brunswick, and Nova Scotia. Manitoba joined Canada in 1870, British Columbia in 1871, and Prince Edward Island in 1873. The boundary of Labrador shown is the present one, which was established by the Privy Council in 1927.

Government of Canada would not allow him to keep all his land.

Bennett travelled round Newfoundland trying to persuade people to join the anti-Confederates. He said that Canada wanted to have Newfoundland's minerals, forests, and fisheries, and that confederation would bring higher taxes and higher prices. He claimed that all young men in Newfoundland would be forced to join the Canadian army or navy and many of them would be killed fighting the United States. Moreover, the great railroads which would be built from Vancouver to Halifax would not help Newfoundland because it was an island.

Carter and Shea claimed that Bennett was exaggerating. However, they were not successful in persuading the people that confederation would bring prosperity to Newfoundland. When an election was held to decide whether or not Newfoundland should join Canada, the people voted for the anti-Confederates. Ambrose Shea himself was defeated by Bennett in the District of Placentia and St. Mary's. Soon afterwards Bennett became Prime Minister.

Explore and Discover

1. Try to find as many reasons as you can why some people in the British colonies thought the colonies should unite. What did Britain and the United States think of such a union?
2. Divide your class into two groups to represent the Confederates and the anti-Confederates. The leader of the Confederates will be Ambrose Shea and the leader of the anti-Confederates will be Charles Bennett. Then hold a debate on the topic: *Newfoundland should join the Confederation of Canada.*

34   The Railway

For fifty years after Newfoundland was granted Responsible Government, there were prosperous times as well as poverty. As had been the case ever since Newfoundland's discovery, there were years when fish was plentiful and could be dried, when crops grew well, and when the price of fish in foreign markets was high. There were other years when fish was scarce, when the weather was bad, when potatoes rotted in the ground, and when other countries did not buy Newfoundland fish.

Still, conditions in Newfoundland slowly improved. There was now much less lawlessness than there had been before the coming of Representative Government. Slowly, roads were linking up the principal settlements. Schools and churches had been built in most communities. Such towns as Harbour Grace, Carbonear, Trinity, Bonavista, Fogo, Twillingate, Grand Bank, and Harbour Breton had become flourishing centres of trade. St. John's, the business centre of Newfoundland, was a prosperous town of twenty thousand people. From its busy harbour, food, clothing, fishery supplies, and many other things that the people needed were carried by schooners all round the coast.

It was during those years that Newfoundland's geographical position became very important. Newfoundland is the part of North America closest to Europe. When it was decided to lay a telegraph cable across the Atlantic Ocean, Newfoundland was chosen as its landing place. Laying the cable was a very

When the railway was begun, some Newfoundlanders were afraid that they would lose their lands and homes to it. Other men feared that the railway would be too expensive to build. The first train trip across the island from St. John's to Port-aux-Basques was made seventeen years later in 1898.

difficult task. Finally in 1866, after many attempts, the *Great Eastern* landed the cable at Heart's Content. Now messages which used to take a month to cross the ocean could be sent in seconds.

While Newfoundland held a very important place in trans-Atlantic communication, within the island itself communication was a big problem. Boats could travel along the coast, but they could not reach the interior of the island. The coastline was so long and the settlements were so scattered that the cost of building roads was more than the government could afford. However the settlements in the interior had to be linked before Newfoundland's resources of minerals and timber could be developed. For as long as the fishery was the only industry, there would always be times of scarcity.

Thus the government decided to build a railroad across the

131

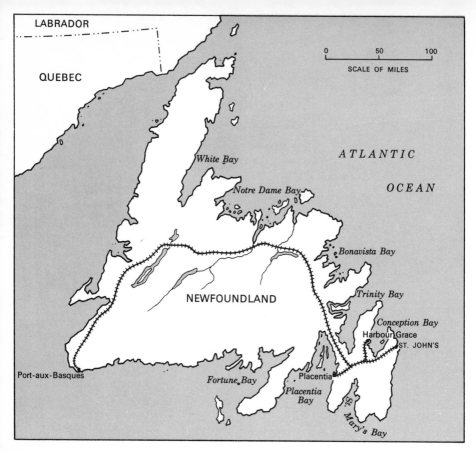

The railway was begun in 1881, and lines were built to Harbour Grace and Placentia. In 1890 the Reid Newfoundland Company took over the building of the railway and finished the line to Port-aux-Basques. Today the railway and coastal steamers are operated by the Canadian National Railways.

island. This was a very big task because Newfoundland's population was small and money was scarce. Nevertheless in 1881 a contract was signed and work began. Within a few years the railway lines from St. John's to Harbour Grace and Placentia were built. At that time the contractor had no more money and work stopped.

Robert Reid now undertook to complete the railway for $15,600 and five thousand acres of land for each mile of track built. After three more years the line was completed to Port-aux-Basques. Reid agreed to run the railway and to take charge of eight coastal steamers which would carry passengers, mail, and freight to outports not reached by the railway. He also agreed to operate the dry dock which had recently been built in St. John's.

The railway and the coastal boats were operated by the Reid Newfoundland Company for about twenty years. Then, because the Company was losing money, the government took over and continued the operation until 1949, when the Newfoundland Railway became part of the giant Canadian National Railways system.

The Newfoundland Railway brought about many of the things which the government had hoped it would achieve. It linked the West Coast to the East, making possible the development of the paper industry at Grand Falls and Corner Brook, the airport at Gander, and the lead and zinc mines at Buchans. On the other hand, the government had gone deeply into debt to build the railway, and this was to have serious results later.

Explore and Discover

1. With the help of your teacher, try to find out what reasons some people had against building the railway. Then divide your class into two groups and hold a debate on the topic: *Newfoundland should build a railway.*

2. Why was Newfoundland chosen as the place to land the first telegraph cable across the Atlantic?

3. What was the main way of travelling in Newfoundland before the building of the railway? How do Newfoundland people travel today?

35 The Great Fire and the Bank Crash

While the government of Newfoundland was borrowing every cent it could to complete the railway, two disasters occurred which made life very difficult for many people.

The first of these disasters was a great fire which, in 1892, destroyed nearly all of St. John's. The fire started in a barn near the crossing of Freshwater and Pennywell Roads. The city's water supply had been shut off that day while pipes were being repaired. Soon the fire, fanned by a strong wind, was out of control. Sixteen hours later shops, hospitals, churches, and homes had become smouldering ashes. More than eleven thousand people were homeless. Help came from England, from the United States, and from Canada. Soon the town was being rebuilt.

Then came another disaster—the bank crash. The banks of Newfoundland had been badly managed. They had lent large sums of money to the government, which the government could not repay. They themselves had borrowed large sums from the Savings Bank, which they could not repay. Finally they announced that they could no longer operate.

The situation was desperate. All the people who had put their money in the banks were suddenly penniless. All the paper money in Newfoundland became worthless. Cheques

In 1892 a fire broke out in St. John's and raged for sixteen hours. It destroyed almost 2,000 buildings and left over 11,000 people homeless. This photograph shows the terrible damage that had to be repaired. England, Canada, and the United States helped by giving money and materials.

could not be cashed. Businesses could not borrow. It seemed that Newfoundland would be utterly ruined.

Britain was now asked for help. Sir Robert Bond, the Prime Minister, personally borrowed $100,000 to help the Savings Bank. Bond also persuaded banks in England to lend the Newfoundland government enough money to allow its work to continue. Soon arrangements were made for the Bank of Montreal, the Bank of Nova Scotia, and the Royal Bank of Canada to replace the banks which had failed.

One man, Sir William Whiteway, thought that the best way to overcome the difficulties Newfoundland now faced was to enter Confederation. A delegation went to Ottawa to talk with the Canadian government, but the terms offered by Canada were not generous enough for Newfoundland. If Canada had been more generous at that time, perhaps Newfoundland would have become part of Canada then. But as matters turned out, the people of Newfoundland were angry that Whiteway had suggested joining Canada. At the next election he was defeated.

The bank crash had been even more serious than the great fire, but Newfoundland survived both disasters and remained independent. This was in large part due to the hard work and patriotism of Sir Robert Bond.

Explore and Discover

1. Ask your teacher to read to you the story of the fire of 1892 from *The History of Newfoundland* by D. W. Prowse.
2. Imagine that you were living in St. John's in 1892 and write a story telling about the great fire.
3. Think of all the problems that would arise if people had no money at all. How could they buy and sell goods?
4. List three reasons why Newfoundland was able to survive the bank crash.
5. Why did that particular time turn out to be a bad one for Whiteway to suggest that Newfoundland join Canada?

36 Coaker and the Fishermen's Protective Union

When Newfoundland had been granted Responsible Government, it had been thought that all the people of Newfoundland would take part in the government. Fifty years later, however, it seemed that the working people were playing a less important part in the government than they should be. It was true that every man who was over twenty-one years of age could vote, but those who were elected often seemed to represent merchants, businessmen, and lawyers, whereas most of the people of Newfoundland were fishermen and loggers. Moreover, the working people were little better off now than they had been fifty years earlier.

One man who wanted to improve this state of affairs was Sir Edward Morris. In 1907 he formed a party called the People's Party, and two years later he became Prime Minister. He hoped to help the poor people by passing laws that would provide better schools and hospitals, as well as old age pensions and other benefits. Almost all the voters in the Avalon Peninsula and in southern Newfoundland supported Morris, but he got very few votes in the north, where the people supported William Ford Coaker.

William Coaker was born in St. John's, and at the age of sixteen he was manager of a store at Pike's Arm near Herring

Neck. He was very interested in the life of the fishermen and started a night school to help them. There they learned to read and write so that they would be able to keep their accounts properly. He was also interested in farming and soon started a farm on an island near Twillingate, which became one of the best in Newfoundland.

Here on his farm he read a great deal and thought about how he could help the working people of Newfoundland. Finally he decided that he would form a great union of all the fishermen, loggers, sealers, and other workers.

About the same time that Sir Edward Morris formed the People's Party, Coaker organized the first branch of his union at Herring Neck. From then on he travelled along the East Coast, forming other branches. After six years, the union had a membership of twenty thousand.

Coaker called his organization the Fishermen's Protective Union. He told the members that in the past they had been robbed when they bought their supplies, when they sold their fish, and when they paid taxes to support dishonest civil servants. He said that if they were to improve this situation, they had to own their own shops, sell their own fish, and take control of the government.

In the years that followed, the Fishermen's Protective Union built ships and a shipyard and established an import and export company. A light and power company was started, which brought electricity to the Bonavista Peninsula. The F.P.U. built their headquarters at Port Union and published their own newspaper, the *Fishermen's Advocate*.

In the election of 1913 Coaker supported the Liberal Party led by Sir Robert Bond. Nine of Coaker's followers stood for election as Liberal candidates and eight were successful, but the People's Party won the election. Later, after Sir Robert

Corner Brook, the second largest city in Newfoundland, has a population of about 26,000. It is an important industrial centre, having one of the largest pulp and paper mills in the world. The making of cement, gypsum, and fish products are other important industries. Many tourists visit Corner Brook because the Humber River is one of the best salmon rivers in Newfoundland. An agricultural fair is held in Corner Brook each year.

Bond had retired, Coaker supported the new Liberal leader, Sir Richard Squires.

For the next ten years the F.P.U. played an important part in the government of Newfoundland. During that time laws were passed to improve the working conditions of loggers and sealers and an attempt was made to improve the lot of the fishermen. Coaker helped Squires in getting a paper mill built at Corner Brook. But Coaker's plans for free and compulsory education, for old age pensions, for a minimum wage law, and for improving the quality and marketing of fish came to nothing.

At first Coaker succeeded in stirring up the fishermen to help themselves and to take an active part in government. But the fishermen who were elected to the Assembly proved no better than the people who had represented them earlier. Coaker's dream that all the workers of Newfoundland should work together to make people happy and prosperous was a magnificent one, but it remained a dream.

Explore and Discover

1. What is a union? With the help of your teacher try to find out whether any unions exist in Newfoundland today, and if so, what they are.
2. List as many reasons as you can find why Coaker decided to form the Fishermen's Protective Union.
3. Make a list of the things that Coaker and the F.P.U. achieved, and another list of the things they failed to achieve.
4. Imagine that you were a fisherman who had gone to Coaker's night school. Write a letter to a friend explaining why you are going to join the F.P.U.

37 The First World War

When Britain declared war on Germany in 1914, Newfoundland, being a British colony, was at war as well. The war lasted for four years and cost Newfoundland a great deal, both in lives and in money.

Many young Newfoundlanders crossed the ocean to fight in France: 5,482 joined the Royal Newfoundland Regiment and the Forestry Corps. Many others joined the Royal Navy. Altogether 1,305 men from the Royal Newfoundland Regiment were killed and 2,314 wounded. In the Battle of Beaumont Hamel alone, the Regiment was reduced from 753 to 68 men.

Despite the number of brave men who had volunteered to serve in the army and the navy, the government did not think that Newfoundlanders were doing enough to help win the war. A conscription law was passed which ordered every able-bodied young man to join the army or navy when he was called, whether he wished to or not. Many people were against this law, but could do nothing because no elections were held while the war lasted. However, the war ended before many of the conscripted men were sent overseas.

To train and equip all the soldiers and sailors cost Newfoundland a great deal of money. When the war ended, it was found that Newfoundland had spent $13,000,000. This amount was more than Newfoundland could afford. Moreover, most of the money had been borrowed.

This close-up photograph shows the figures of soldiers on the War Memorial in St. John's. The War Memorial was built in 1924 in memory of the Newfoundland men who lost their lives in battle.

During the war Sir Edward Morris was Prime Minister and William Coaker supported him, because he believed that in wartime everyone should work together. Morris, however, often had to go to London, where the Prime Ministers of all British colonies which had Responsible Governments met with the British government to plan the best way to fight the war. In the end Morris decided to remain in England and became a member of the British House of Lords.

As soon as the war was over, the parties in the Assembly decided that they could no longer work together. An election was held to decide who would become Prime Minister. Sir Richard Squires, who was supported by William Coaker, won the election.

Explore and Discover

1. Why did Newfoundland take part in the First World War?
2. What does conscription mean?
3. Why do you think some Newfoundlanders were against conscription? Write down the reasons that you find.
4. Why do you think the Newfoundland parties worked together so well during the war? Why were elections held when the war was over?

38 Labrador

During Governor Palliser's time the British government had given the coast of Labrador to Newfoundland. Palliser had tried very hard to keep settlers from going to Labrador, but he had not succeeded. As the years passed, trappers, traders, and fishermen began to make their homes in Labrador. In the far north the Moravian missionaries built mission stations and converted the Eskimos to Christianity.

Soon more and more Newfoundland fishermen began to go to Labrador for the summer months. Some of them went in schooners, on which they lived during the fishing season. Others went as passengers on schooners or coastal steamers and fished from the shore. Most of the fishermen returned to Newfoundland in the autumn, but some of them stayed behind and settled on the coast. Some Indians, too, who trapped in the interior, set up villages near the trading posts on the coast.

For many years life on the coast of Labrador was like life on the coast of Newfoundland before the coming of Responsible Government. There was a small population scattered in tiny coves and harbours along the many miles of coast. There were few schools, and only rarely did missionaries visit the isolated villages. There were no courts or policemen. The only way to travel was by boat in the summer and by dog team in the winter. Every summer the population grew much larger as hundreds of Newfoundland schooners carried thousands of fishermen to the coast. In the winter, when all the summer visitors had gone, many of the permanent settlers left the isolated and rocky headlands and moved to winter quarters in the sheltered bays.

Slowly the Eskimos began to move to the far north, where the Moravians had built their mission stations. There they

In this photograph a healthy Eskimo baby is being given a ride. Even though today many Eskimo children go to school, the girls learn early to look after smaller children, to cook, and to sew. The boys learn to throw harpoons and to hunt with rifles. Often the toys they play with are made for them by adults and show what their duties at home are. For the boys, weapons are made from bone and ivory. Dolls as well as cooking pots are made for the girls.

received some schooling and medical care, as well as food when starvation threatened them. In the south the settlers fished, hunted for seals and sea birds, and trapped furbearing animals. Life was difficult, and the hardships were many.

Eventually the Newfoundland government began to take an interest in the settlers on the Labrador coast. Soon schools and churches were being built. Then came the Grenfell Mission, whose work we have already discussed.

For many years people thought that Labrador was important only because fish was plentiful in the coastal waters, salmon lived in the rivers, and seals could be hunted on the ice floes off the coast. But Labrador has other great riches. There are vast forests, rich deposits of minerals, and mighty rivers that can be harnessed to produce electric power. For a long time these riches were ignored, partly because the long, cold winters hindered development, and partly because ice blocked the coast for many months each year and made the shipment of minerals and forest products difficult.

When men did begin to think of ways in which Labrador could be developed, a serious problem arose. The Canadian province of Quebec claimed Labrador. The Government of Canada agreed with this claim, insisting that inland Labrador had always been part of Quebec and that Newfoundland owned only the coast, that is, a strip of land not more than a mile wide along the ocean.

For many years Canada and Newfoundland argued about the ownership of this valuable territory. At last the Judicial Committee of the Privy Council in England, the highest court in the British Empire, was asked to settle the quarrel.

Lawyers from Newfoundland and from Canada went to London. For many weeks they presented their evidence and arguments. Then on March 1, 1927, the Privy Council an-

Churchill Falls is almost twice the size of Niagara Falls. At present an underground powerhouse is being built 1,000 feet below the rock surface. When it is finished, the falls will be the site of the province's largest hydro-electric plant and will supply electricity to the Atlantic coast of both Canada and the United States. Called the Grand Falls before 1965, the falls as well as the Hamilton River were renamed after the late Sir Winston Churchill.

nounced its decision that Newfoundland owned the coast of Labrador, and that the coast included all that part of Labrador through which flowed rivers that drained into the Atlantic Ocean. Newfoundland had won her case, gaining territory nearly three times as large as the island of Newfoundland itself.

This was a very important victory, for now the great wealth of Labrador is being developed. Scientists and engineers have discovered ways of mining the vast deposits of iron ore at Labrador City and Wabush. A railway has been built to carry the iron to the port of Sept Iles. Plans are being made to harvest timber and manufacture pulpwood. The most exciting development of all is the harnessing of the mighty Churchill

Labrador City was developed in order to mine the iron ore deposits found in that area. It was built by the Iron Ore Company of Canada, and today most of its 7,000 inhabitants work for the company. It is a modern, well-planned community, having three schools and a Salvation Army hospital.

Falls and the transformation of the great power of those falls into electricity.

Modern towns are now being built in Labrador. They have excellent schools and hospitals. As on the island of Newfoundland, many small, isolated villages can be found on the coast, but slowly changes are taking place that will give all the people the opportunity to live comfortable lives.

Coastal boat services still link the coast with the island of Newfoundland, but there are also airplane connections with all parts of the world. In the winter snowmobiles are replacing dog teams. Highways are being built, and there is even a hope that some day a tunnel under the Strait of Belle Isle may link Labrador and Newfoundland. The government has recognized these changes by announcing that the name of the province is no longer "Newfoundland", but "Newfoundland and Labrador".

Explore and Discover

1. Why is Labrador a very important part of the Province of Newfoundland and Labrador?

2. The boundary between the Province of Newfoundland and Labrador and the Province of Quebec runs along the "height of land", or watershed. With the help of your teacher, make a clay or plaster model to show what a height of land is.

3. From newspapers or magazines find out as much as you can about the development of Churchill Falls. If you write to the Churchill Falls (Labrador) Corporation, 1 Westmount Square, Montreal, they may be able to help you with your project. Perhaps you could make a Churchill Falls scrapbook.

4. From books in your school, home, or public library, try to learn about the way that Eskimos live. If you are able to find pictures of Eskimos, perhaps you could make an Eskimo scrapbook. Otherwise, you could write down what you have learned about them.

39　The Amulree Report

During the war there had been great prosperity because New-foundland products were in great demand and prices were very high. After the war, however, life became more difficult. The price of fish and of other Newfoundland products fell lower and lower. Soon many people were unemployed and many went hungry.

In St. John's a large public meeting turned into a riot. A crowd of nearly ten thousand people attacked the Colonial Building, where the Assembly was in session. They broke all the windows and threatened the Prime Minister and other members of the government. Then the mob broke into shops and stores. Finally, a ship of the Royal Navy had to be called to restore order.

Since the government was now very unpopular, a general election was called. The Prime Minister, Sir Richard Squires, and all but two of his followers were defeated. The new Prime Minister was F. C. Alderdice. He had promised that if he were elected, he would ask the British government to appoint a Royal Commission to study Newfoundland's problems and to suggest ways to solve them.

A Royal Commission was soon appointed. It was headed by Lord Amulree, who came to Newfoundland and in a short time presented a report. The report said that Newfoundland had been badly governed and that too much money had been

By 1932 the depression was forcing the government to spend as little money as possible. Many people had no work and were discontented. Here you can see the crowd in front of the Colonial Building after the riot.

spent. It claimed that taxes for the poor people were too high and not high enough for the wealthy people. It suggested that fishermen should be paid in cash for their fish and not in supplies, as had been the case in the past. The report also said that in Newfoundland's Civil Service men were given jobs not because they were able to do them well, but because they were friends or relatives of members of the government.

For these reasons Lord Amulree recommended that Newfoundland should have a different kind of government. Responsible Government, he said, should be replaced by Commission of Government. Under Commission of Government no one would be elected. A governor and six commissioners would be appointed by the British government. The governor and the three most important commissioners would be British. Britain would also look after Newfoundland's budget and supply money to the government when necessary.

151

Lord Amulree had made many mistakes in his report. He did not understand the great problems caused by scattered settlement and lack of communication in Newfoundland. He thought that the fishery would always be Newfoundland's only important industry and that the railway, on which a great deal of money had been spent, had not been needed. He did not understand that the real reason for Newfoundland's troubles was the depression.

The depression is the name we give to the years of scarcity before the Second World War. In Canada, in the United States, and in Europe thousands of men were unemployed. Thousands went hungry. No one had money to spend, and no one could buy fish or any other product from Newfoundland. As a result, Newfoundlanders had no money with which to buy food from other countries or to pay taxes to the government.

Even though there were many mistakes in Lord Amulree's report, most Newfoundlanders agreed with it. They blamed their government for the hardships they were suffering and welcomed the Commission of Government.

Explore and Discover

1. Discuss how the people of Newfoundland today can bring about a change in the way that they are governed.
2. Find out what a Royal Commission is. Why did Alderdice promise to bring a Royal Commission to Newfoundland?
3. Make a list of the good suggestions that the Royal Commission made. Then make a list of the mistakes Lord Amulree made.

40 Commission of Government

The Commission of Government ruled Newfoundland for fifteen years, beginning in 1934. During the first six years of this period, while the depression continued, very few improvements were made. Then came the Second World War and a return to prosperity.

The Commission put into practice many of Coaker's ideas in order to improve the fisheries. They tried to persuade fishermen to be more careful in preparing the fish so that it would be a clean and wholesome product that customers would buy. Laws were made to prevent salmon and lobsters from being completely destroyed. The price of fishery supplies was lowered and inspectors were appointed to enforce these laws.

The Commission was also anxious to improve the educational system in Newfoundland. They made every child between the ages of seven and fourteen attend school and provided free school books. Plans were made to train more teachers and to build more schools.

The health of Newfoundlanders was just as serious a problem as their education. The Commission therefore made manufacturers add vitamins to all the margarine and flour sold in Newfoundland. They gave free chocolate milk and cod liver oil to all school children. A sanatorium was built where tuberculous patients could have free treatment. Also, cottage hospitals were built in many outports. The patients of these hospitals

This cottage hospital in Burgeo is one of several established by the Commission of Government. Cottage hospitals were built to give low-cost medical treatment to Newfoundland's scattered and isolated communities.

paid a very low fee each year and then received free medical treatment for the rest of the year. Teachers and parents were encouraged to train children in good health habits.

The Commission also began to set up a better Civil Service. This was very important, since in the past people had been employed because they practised a particular religion or were relatives or friends of people in the government. The Commission believed that any person employed to work for the government should be the one best able to do the work. They therefore set up competitions, which anyone could enter, from which civil servants would be chosen.

154

Although the Commission did many important things, they did not like to spend money. They did not try to develop new industries or to improve roads and other forms of communication.

Moreover, the Commission of Government ruled Newfoundland as if they were dictators. That is, they could do as they wished without asking the people of Newfoundland whether or not they agreed. They could pass laws, collect taxes, and spend Newfoundlanders' money in any way they liked, but the people of Newfoundland had no say in what they did. Newfoundlanders had given up the power which they had had under Responsible Government.

Explore and Discover

1. Discuss with your teacher how the cottage hospital plan works, and write down what you learn.
2. Do you think that the members of the Commission of Government were wise to make all the children between the ages of seven and fourteen attend school? Why?
3. In what ways were the members of the Commission of Government like dictators?
4. What were some of the good things that the Commission of Government achieved?

41   The Second World War

The Second World War, which began in 1939 and lasted for six years, brought great prosperity to Newfoundland. Fish, timber, and minerals were in great demand and prices rose. Wages, too, increased rapidly. Earlier the government had spent large sums of money to support the unemployed; now very little money had to be spent. Soon Newfoundland was able to offer money to Britain to help fight the war.

Thousands of young Newfoundlanders volunteered to serve overseas with the British forces. They served in the Army, the Navy, the Air Force, and the Forestry Corps.

Although the men who served in the Merchant Navy were not members of the regular armed forces, they played an important part in winning the war, since they carried food and war supplies across the ocean to Britain. This was very dangerous work. There were many submarines in the Atlantic Ocean waiting to sink supply ships with torpedoes. Hundreds of ships were sunk, many very close to the shores of Newfoundland. One ship was sunk at the Bell Island pier and several others were sunk nearby. The *Caribou,* a Newfoundland coastal steamer, was sunk while crossing the Cabot Strait from Sydney to Port-aux-Basques.

Newfoundland had always occupied a very important position in all forms of trans-Atlantic communication. The first trans-Atlantic telegraph cable had been landed at Heart's

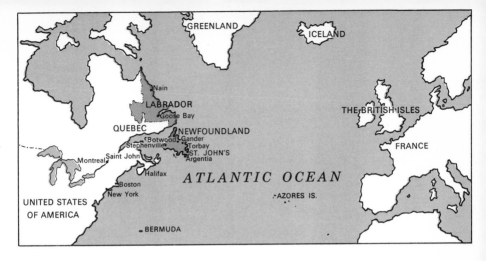

This map shows the strategic importance of Newfoundland in trans-Atlantic communication. During World War II the province's airports were among the busiest in the world, sending men, materials, and airplanes to Britain.

Content, and in the years that followed, many other cables had been landed on the East Coast. Marconi had received the first wireless message across the Atlantic in Cabot Tower on Signal Hill. When men had first dreamed of flying across the Atlantic, they had made Newfoundland their base, and it was from Newfoundland that the first trans-Atlantic flight had been made by Alcock and Brown in 1919.

During the Second World War there were many submarines in Newfoundland waters. If you study a map, you will see that ships setting out for British ports from the harbours of Montreal, Halifax, Saint John, Boston, New York, and other harbours along the Atlantic Coast pass very close to Newfoundland.

The governments of Britain, the United States, and Canada realized that Newfoundland's position was important. Soon after war broke out, divisions of the Canadian army, navy, and air force came to Newfoundland. The airports at Torbay and Gander were built. Airplanes from these bases helped to protect the ships crossing the Atlantic.

The United States government now asked Britain for permission to build bases in Newfoundland. The British government granted this request without asking the Newfoundland people whether or not they agreed. The Commission of Government, of course, knew of the agreement, but they did not represent the Newfoundland people.

As a result of the agreement American air force bases were established at St. John's, Stephenville, and Goose Bay, and a naval base was built at Argentia. The construction of the bases

Gander airport was hastily built to help the war effort. In 1950, when the government decided to establish a proper community near the airport, there were over 3,000 people living in old army buildings. Today Gander is a prosperous town, and Gander International Airport, serving the airlines of many nations, is called the "Crossroads of the World".

provided employment for many Newfoundlanders and added nearly forty million dollars a year to Newfoundland's budget. Even after the war, these bases continued to operate for some time. Since then the development of long-range rockets and missiles has made the air force bases less important. Today only the naval base at Argentia is still used.

Although there was great prosperity during the war, the members of Commission of Government were very cautious and put large sums of money in the bank. Instead of using the money to develop Newfoundland, they said that they would spend it after the war.

Explore and Discover

1. Why was Newfoundland's geographical position very important during the Second World War?
2. What changes took place in Newfoundland during the war?
3. Find out as much as you can about early attempts to fly the Atlantic.
4. Ask your teacher to read to you, or to find a book for you in which you can read the story of the *Great Eastern*.

42   The National Convention

In 1934 the people of Newfoundland had been promised that as soon as conditions improved and the Commission of Government was no longer needed, the people themselves could choose the kind of government they wanted. For several years before the end of the war, some men had been saying that it was again time for Newfoundlanders to govern themselves. As soon as the war ended, the British government asked Newfoundlanders what should be done.

The first step was to bring together representatives of all the people to discuss the problem. Elections were therefore held, and the men who were elected came to St. John's to form what was known as the National Convention. The National Convention was to decide whether the Commission of Government should continue or whether there should be a return to Responsible Government.

Perhaps because there was prosperity, the people of Newfoundland did not seem to be very interested in the election. Only one out of every five adults voted. Among the men elected was Mr. Joseph Roberts Smallwood. He did not believe that the Commission of Government should continue to rule Newfoundland, or that Newfoundland should have Responsible Government. He thought that Confederation with Canada would be the answer to Newfoundland's problems.

The Confederates, led by Mr. Smallwood, claimed that

Mr. Joseph R. Smallwood was a strong supporter of Newfoundland's joining Confederation. He became Premier in 1949 and has continued to lead the Liberal Party and the government of the province since that time.

Newfoundland was too small to remain independent. Newfoundland's population would not be able to develop the resources of the country. After a few years under Responsible Government, they said, Newfoundlanders would once again have to ask Britain for help.

They pointed out also that within Confederation Newfoundland would be part of a large and prosperous nation. Newfoundlanders would receive family allowances, old age pensions, and other benefits that the Newfoundland government alone could not afford to pay. Also, within Confederation there would be money for roads, bridges, wharves, and other kinds of public works.

Moreover, the Confederates claimed that this was a good time to make a bargain with Canada, since the war had proved that Newfoundland was important. Canada was anxious that Newfoundlanders should enter Confederation. On the other hand, the British government wanted to be sure that Newfoundland would never again need Britain's help.

However, there were many Newfoundlanders who were anti-Confederates. They were proud men and women who remembered that Newfoundlanders had struggled for centuries

161

to build and keep their homes and that the fight for Responsible Government had been difficult. They knew that the conditions that had brought the Commission of Government to Newfoundland had not been the fault of Responsible Government but had been caused by a world-wide depression. They wanted Newfoundland to return to Responsible Government. Then the members of this government, representing the people of Newfoundland, could talk with the Canadian government about Confederation.

The National Convention lasted two years. During that time there were many angry debates, which the people of Newfoundland heard on the radio. Mr. Smallwood spoke often and persuaded many people that it was a good idea to enter Confederation. The majority of the National Convention, however, were anti-Confederates. Finally it was decided that the people of Newfoundland should be asked to vote in a referendum to say whether they wanted Commission of Government or Responsible Government. They would not be asked to say whether or not they favoured Confederation.

Explore and Discover

1. Why was the National Convention elected?
2. What did the Convention decide to do? Why was Confederation not to be put on the referendum ballot?
3. As a class project, hold a debate on Confederation. Divide your class into two sides, one in favour of Confederation and the other in favour of Responsible Government. Let each person make a short speech supporting his side. Then take a vote. Ask your teacher to act as chairman.

43 Confederation

Mr. Smallwood and the Confederates were angry when the Convention made this decision, because they thought that Newfoundlanders should be given a chance to say whether or not they wished to join Canada. They therefore prepared a petition that they persuaded 50,000 people to sign. This petition, which asked that Confederation with Canada be added to the referendum ballot, was sent to the British government.

The supporters of Responsible Government also prepared a petition which was sent to the British government. This petition asked that the decision of the National Convention should not be changed.

The British government wanted Newfoundland to join Canada. Britain thought that the many Newfoundlanders who supported Mr. Smallwood should be given the chance to vote for the kind of government they wanted. It therefore accepted the petition of the Confederates and announced that the referendum would give the people of Newfoundland three choices: Commission of Government, Responsible Government, or Confederation with Canada.

Before the referendum was held, both Confederates and anti-Confederates toured Newfoundland by car, train, boat, and airplane. Each side tried to persuade the people to vote in its favour.

The Federal Parliament Buildings overlook the Ottawa River. In the background is the Interprovincial Bridge that links Ottawa with Hull. Many tourists from Canada and overseas visit Parliament Hill each year in July and August to see the colourful Changing of the Guard ceremony. In May Parliament Hill is covered with thousands of tulips.

When the ballots were counted after the election, it was found that the largest number of people had voted for Responsible Government, a slightly smaller number for Confederation, and the smallest number for Commission of Government.

Though the largest number of votes had been cast for Responsible Government, the number was not large enough to make a majority. The British government therefore decided that a second referendum would be held. This time Commission of Government would not be listed as one of the choices.

The people would vote either for Responsible Government or for Confederation.

Once again, as preparations for voting were made, Confederates and anti-Confederates worked hard to bring people to their side. There was a great deal of bad feeling between the two parties.

When the voting took place, the Confederates won by a very small margin. Newfoundlanders, who twice before had refused to join Canada, had now changed their minds. The man largely responsible for this change was Mr. J. R. Smallwood.

A delegation led by Mr. Smallwood went to Ottawa, where the terms of union between Canada and Newfoundland were negotiated. Finally on March 31, 1949 Newfoundland became the tenth province of Canada.

In the foreground a former Prime Minister of Canada, Louis St. Laurent, and the Chairman of the Newfoundland delegation to Ottawa, A. J. Walsh, are signing the Terms of Union of Canada and Newfoundland in 1949. Mr. Walsh was named the first Lieutenant-Governor of Newfoundland by the Canadian government. Note Mr. J. R. Smallwood, the second from the right.

Some people had feared that within Confederation Newfoundlanders would lose their independence. But in fact each
province keeps its own Responsible Government, which con-
trols all provincial matters. Each province also elects representatives to sit in the Canadian House of Commons at Ottawa.
The House of Commons is the most important part of the
Government of Canada, or the federal government, as it is
usually called. Newfoundland elects seven members to the
House of Commons.

Explore and Discover

1. Why did the British government add Confederation to the referendum ballot?
2. Why did a second referendum have to be held? Why was Commission of Government dropped from the ballot?
3. Try to find out in what areas of government Newfoundland still
   keeps its independence, even though it has joined Canada.
4. How does Newfoundland take part in the federal government?

44 Since Confederation

Shortly after the Confederation agreement was signed, elections were held to decide who would form the provincial government. The Liberal Party won the election, and its leader, Mr. Smallwood, became Premier.

Since then all elections have had the same result. Perhaps the people of Newfoundland are still grateful to Mr. Smallwood for his part in bringing about Confederation. Most Newfoundlanders are proud to be citizens of a young, prosperous nation that is blessed with an abundance of resources and has a very bright future.

Confederation has brought prosperity to Newfoundland. The federal government has given money for the building of roads, wharves, and breakwaters. Community services such as electricity, water, and sewerage have been improved, as well as harbours and airports. Newfoundland has been able to build larger and better schools and to establish a new university. It has been possible to develop Newfoundland's rich resources more fully.

Moreover, family allowances, old age pensions, and unemployment insurance have brought security to many Newfoundlanders who had never known security before.

It would have taken much longer to do these things if Newfoundland had remained a separate Dominion. They

The Confederation Building is a striking landmark in St. John's. A full picture of it, showing its location in the capital, appears on the next page. It has been the home of the Government of Newfoundland and Labrador since 1960. It is an example of the rapid growth of the city since Newfoundland joined Canada.

have been possible because Canada is a democracy. In every democratic country the people pay taxes to the government. Those who earn a great deal of money pay high taxes, while those who earn little money pay low taxes. The government spends the money it collects to help all the people. It tries to share the wealth of the country equally.

Likewise in Confederation the wealthier provinces pay more taxes to the federal government than the poorer provinces pay. The federal government then tries to share the money it collects in such a way that all Canadians receive equal benefits.

Since Confederation, Newfoundlanders have received from the federal government more money than they have paid to it

168

in taxes. However, Newfoundland has brought much to Canada in exchange for this help. Newfoundland's 150,000 square miles of territory are rich in minerals, forests, and waterpower. She has some of the richest fishing grounds in the world. Newfoundland has also added 500,000 people to Canada's population and is a valuable market for Canadian food products and manufactured goods. When all Newfoundland's resources are fully developed, Newfoundlanders should be able to give more than they receive.

St. John's is one of the oldest settlements in North America, its site having been discovered on June 24, 1497 and named after St. John the Baptist. Today it is a modern and prosperous capital. The government of the province sits in the Confederation Building, and Memorial University, Newfoundland's centre of education, is on the outskirts of the city.

Explore and Discover

1. Draw a map of Canada and colour each province differently. Find out when each province joined Confederation and write the date under its name.

2. How does the federal government try to share the wealth of Canada?

3. Find out the names of the member of the federal parliament for your area and of the member of the provincial parliament. What duties to the people of your district does each of these men have?

4. Ask your parents, your teacher, and any other people whom you know what changes have taken place in Newfoundland since 1949. Then make a list of them.

5. Discuss, and then write down all the ways in which Confederation has been a benefit to Newfoundland.

6. Try to find out what projects the Government of Newfoundland is planning in which it will need the help of the Government of Canada.

A SELECT BIBLIOGRAPHY OF THE HISTORY OF NEWFOUNDLAND AND LABRADOR

Books noted ⊙ are suitable for independent pupil reading. Books noted * are especially recommended for teacher use.

Unfortunately many of these books are now out of print. The date of copyright is a good guide in this regard. However, some of the titles may still be available in your local library.

Ammon, Charles G., *Newfoundland, the Forgotten Island*, Doubleday Publishers, 1944.

Anspach, Lewis A., *A History of the Island of Newfoundland and the Coast of Labrador*, 1819.

Blackall, William W., *The Early Story of Newfoundland, St. John's*, 1918.

Bonnycastle, Sir Richard H., *Newfoundland in 1842*, 1842.

⊙ Briffet, Frances B., *Little Stories about Newfoundland*, 1929.

⊙ Briffet, Frances B., *More Stories of Newfoundland*, 1939.

⊙ Briffet, Frances B., *The Story of Newfoundland and Labrador*, J. M. Dent & Sons (Canada) Ltd., 1949.

Brown, Patrick W., *Where the Fishers Go—Story of Labrador*, 1909.

Cabot, William B., *In Northern Labrador*, 1912.

Chadwick, Saint John, *Newfoundland: Island into Province*, Macmillan Company of Canada Ltd., 1966.

⊙ Cochrane, James A., *Story of Newfoundland*, 1938.

* Crouse, Nellis M., *LeMoyne D'Iberville: Soldier of New France*, Ryerson Press, 1954.

* *Dictionary of Canadian Biography, Vol. I*, pp. 1000-1700, University of Toronto Press, 1966.

⊙ Donaldson, Lois, *Newfoundland in Stories and Pictures*, George J. McLeod Ltd., 1944.

Ellis, Frank, *Canada's Flying Heritage*, University of Toronto Press, 1954.

⊙ English, Leo E. F., *Outline of Newfoundland History*, 1929.

* Ganong, William F., *Crucial Maps in the Early Cartography and Place Nomenclature of the Atlantic Coast of Canada*, University of Toronto Press, 1964.

* Grenfell, Sir Wilfred T., *Forty Years for Labrador*, 1932.

* Grenfell, Sir Wilfred T., *Labrador, the Country and the People*, Macmillan Company of Canada Ltd., 1909.

* Grenfell, Sir Wilfred T., *A Labrador Doctor—Autobiography*, Hodder and Stoughten, 1948.

* Grenfell, Sir Wilfred T., *The Romance of Labrador*, 1934.

* Gunn, Gertrude, *The Political History of Newfoundland*, University of Toronto Press, 1966.

Harvey, Moses, *Newfoundland as it is in 1894*, 1894.

Harvey, Moses, *Newfoundland at the Beginning of the Twentieth Century*, 1901.

* Harvey, Moses, and Hatton, J., *Newfoundland, the Oldest British Colony: its History, its Present Condition, and its Prospects in the Future*, 1883.

* Howley, Michael F., *Ecclesiastical History of Newfoundland*, 1888.

* Innis, Harold A., *The Cod Fisheries, the History of an International Economy*, McGill University Press, 1940.

* Jones, Gwyn, *The Norse Atlantic Saga*, Oxford University Press, 1964.

⊙ Leechman, Douglas, *Native Tribes of Canada*, W. J. Gage Ltd., 1957.

⊙ Lewis, W., *Newfoundland, Sentinel of the Atlantic*, Moyer Division, Vilas Industries Ltd., 1949.

* Lounsbury, R. G., *The British Fishery of Newfoundland, 1634-1763*, 1934.

* Magnusson and Palsson, *The Vinland Sagas*, Copp Clark Publishing Co., 1966.

* McClintock, A. H., *Establishment of Constitutional Government in Newfoundland, 1738-1832*, Longmans (Canada) Ltd., 1941.

McGrath, Sir Patrick T., *Newfoundland in 1911*, 1911.

* McKay, Robert A., *Newfoundland Economic, Diplomatic and Strategic Studies*, Oxford University Press, 1946.

* Mowat, Farley, *Westviking*, McClelland & Stewart Ltd., 1965.

* Murray, Jean, *The Newfoundland Journal of Aaron Thomas*, Longmans (Canada) Ltd., 1968.

Nicholson, Col. G. W. L., *The Fighting Newfoundlander*, The Government of Newfoundland, 1964.

Parker, John, *Newfoundland, Tenth Province of Canada*, 1950.

Pedley, Charles, *The History of Newfoundland*, 1863.

* Prowse, D. W., *The History of Newfoundland*, 1895.

* Reeves, John, *History of the Government of the Island of Newfoundland*, J. Sewell, 1793. (Recently re-issued by the Social Science Research Council and the Humanities Research Council of Canada.)

Rogers, John D., *A Historical Geography of the British Colonies, Vol. V, part IV, Newfoundland*, 1911.

Rowe, F. W., *The Development of Education in Newfoundland*, 1963.

Smallwood, Joseph R. (Ed.), *The Book of Newfoundland, Vols. I and II*, Newfoundland Book Publishers, 1937; *Vols. III and IV*, Newfoundland Book Publishing Ltd., 1967.

Smallwood, Joseph R., *Stories of Newfoundland: Source Book for Teachers*, Newfoundland Gazette.

Tait, Robert H., *Newfoundland, A Summary of the History and Development of Britain's Oldest Colony*, 1939.

Tocque, Philip, *Newfoundland as it was and as it is in 1877*, 1878.

⊙ Williamson, Thames, *North After Seals*, a Puffin Book, Penguin Books, 1946.

* Williamson, T., *The Cabot Voyages and Bristol Discovery*, The Hakluyt Society, 1966.

Young, Ewart, *This Is Newfoundland*, Ryerson Press, 1949.

INDEX

The text of this book is set in 12 on 14 point Baskerville, with questions in 11 on 13 point and chapter titles in 24 point. The book is printed on 60 lb. Century Opaque Litho. Printed and bound in Canada by The Hunter Rose Company.

4   5   6   7   8   9   10   HR   77   76   75   74   73   72   71